GARY COOPER

GARY COOPER

A Pyramid Illustrated History of the Movies

by

RENE JORDAN

General Editor: **TED SENNETT**

PYRAMID

PUBLICATIONS

NEW YORK

GARY COOPER
A Pyramid Illustrated History of the Movies

Copyright © 1974 by Pyramid Communications, Inc.

First edition published March 1974

Pyramid Illustrated History of the Movies

ISBN 0-515-03416-9

Library of Congress Catalog Card Number: 73-21125

Printed in the United States of America

Pyramid Books are published by Pyramid Communications, Inc. Its trademarks, consisting of the word "Pyramid" and the portrayal of a pyramid, are registered in the United States Patent Office.

PYRAMID COMMUNICATIONS, INC.
919 Third Avenue, New York, N.Y. 10022

graphic design by anthony basile

For G. Cain,
who taught me to appreciate Gary Cooper

ACKNOWLEDGMENTS

I wish to express my gratitude to my editor, Ted Sennett, who with unerring perception, deep knowledge of film and inexhaustible patience has guided me through three books.

Photographs: Jerry Vermilye, Movie Star News, Photo Archives, and Penguin Photo Collection.

CONTENTS

THE MAKING OF A HERO

During his thirty-five year reign as a film idol, Gary Cooper faced a movie camera and looked it straight in the eye. It was a far more treacherous villain than any he encountered in over one hundred films. This black, whirring monster could look through him, revealing his thoughts, unmasking any fakery, deflating every trick. In the desperation of the hounded, he had only one weapon: armed with his honesty he confronted the mechanical Medusa. It had turned many contenders into stone, but it turned Cooper into a star.

He learned his lesson early, as a quivering novice. Between takes of *Nevada*, one of his early silent Westerns, he heard Thelma Todd refer to the camera as "the enemy." He never forgot those words and to the very end he respected the one-eyed monster. He never tried to fool it or hoodwink it as he slowly turned into a fine film actor and then into a living incarnation of the hidden longings of his audience, the human stuff that all-American dreams were made of.

Cooper had no formal training as an actor and never learned to project all the way to a second balcony. He played directly to the camera, without a trace of ham in his bone-dry performances. "Don't do something, just stand there," the inverted cliché now reads, but before

it was coined Cooper had developed it into a method.

There are countless stories about directors he drove to anger with his refusal to emote. "He does nothing on the set," Sam Wood said when he first directed him in *Pride of the Yankees*. "You are sure it is the worst performance ever, but then you see the rushes and it is all there on the screen." The camera always saw what the naked eye missed because Cooper acted inside his head and his conviction was disarming, touching, contagious.

During the three-and-a-half decades of his supremacy, stars blazed and consumed themselves, but Cooper continued to shine, stamping his own brand of truth on the most farfetched plots. Ask even the most inarticulate Cooper fan to describe his style and the answer is invariably something like "He was so natural!" The words pinpoint a popular enchantment with the spontaneous and unrehearsed: it is the same emotion of unconditional wonder evoked by a baby grabbing one's finger or a puppy wagging its tail. Doing what comes naturally is regarded instantly as cute, lovable,

even clever. When this form of naturalism is artfully refined into understated acting, the audience marvels, and stars are admired for appearing to do nothing, precisely when they have mastered the hardest of tricks: *being* instead of doing.

"Behavioristic" is a term Gary Cooper would have dismissed as a "sixty-four dollar word," but there is no more accurate way to describe how he behaved, how he *lived* in front of a camera, as if its inquisitive eye were catching him unawares. Paul Muni, John Barrymore, George Arliss: the widely hailed but stage-trained performers of the early talkies now look fussy and mannered whenever they forget the proximity of the camera and concentrate on the hypothetical audience behind it. They tried to establish an immediate rapport with those unseen viewers; the camera, like all ignored intermediaries, took its revenge on them. Their acting has become sermonizing while Cooper's is direct, fresh, even *confessional*.

Cooper, like Garbo, is so reserved and aloof on the screen that he can claim the charm of discretion even in the worst of his early silent melodramas. Ernst Lubitsch, who directed both stars, once jokingly told Garson Kanin that Cooper and Garbo had never made a film together because they were the same person. Then Lubitsch seriously explained that they were essentially photogenic creatures: bland, almost dull, except when a camera was pointed at them.

In their bones, Garbo and Cooper felt that a scrutinizing lens could turn gestures into gesticulation, grins into grimaces. Garbo sometimes insisted on acting behind cardboard partitions, with only the camera peeping through a hole, like an unwelcome visitor. Cooper had such concentration that he did not need the physical isolation: he could turn inward at will, blocking out the rest. He stood alone, as if on the slide of a microscope, waiting for his minimal gestures to be enlarged into revelation.

It is significant to know that Cooper's first goal was to be a political cartoonist, an ambition he achieved indirectly on the screen. He isolated the revealing quirk, magnified the salient trait, then infused the sketch with warmth and humanity, transmuting caricature into character. The few examples left of his artist's work are hopelessly amateurish: he would never have become a Herblock or a Bill Mauldin, yet Cooper used his mind and body as a pencil. He posed in the flesh for a full gallery of recognizable portraits of America in transition, from Sergeant York to Mr. Deeds, from John Doe to Good Sam.

His sharp eye could catch the simple action, the precise bit of exaggeration that would typify a person at a glance. The shifting eyes, the half-suppressed shrug, the smile that comes and goes so fast one wonders if it was a mirage: taken out of context they have been damned as tics or mannerisms, but they were Cooper's ploys in the game of action-reaction. A past master of the two-shot, he had a hairbreadth calculation of what editing could bring out in a performance.

Cooper was the quintessential movie actor, admired and envied by those he looked upon as his betters. "We try, but he *is*," Charles Laughton admitted. "In his heart he is pure," John Barrymore said. "He believes in it." George Cukor put it more clearly and succinctly when interviewed by Gavin Lambert: "Really sincere acting with very few tricks—someone like Gary Cooper—is dismissed with 'Oh, but he is such a simple person, what he is playing is so simple.' Look at it right up close, it is much more than that."

Looking closely at a Cooper performance is like finding pieces of silver long forgotten in last year's winter coat. One keeps discovering the unexpected, for Cooper had planted his surprises in every nook and cranny of the plot, giving his audiences just enough and no more. He often disparaged his craft and

was once heard muttering: "This is surely a silly way to make a living." But he was his own best advocate against the stigma of merely playing himself: "When they say I'm just being me, they don't know how hard it is to be a guy like me."

Cooper was only hinting at how hard it was to fulfill the audience's expectations of him. His films made him the repository of American longings after a lost, perhaps nonexistent innocence. In his key performances, Cooper extolled the grassroots decency of Mr. Deeds, the rustic nobility of Sergeant York, the grossly manipulated goodness of John Doe, and the unswerving sense of justice of Marshal Will Kane in *High Noon*.

It was all done without props, heavy make-up, or subterfuge. His face was naked and sorrowful for all the world to see. It was indeed difficult to be a guy like Cooper: the gentle paladin chasing the long-forgotten dreams of his no-longer adolescent audience. As they sat watching him, they could have detected the most minute smirk of cynicism but there was none: Cooper was true to his calling and he gave the faithful what they had come for.

Cooper fans revelled vicariously in his good will, his uncorruptibility, even when they knew his quest was futile in a hypocritical world. He was to be admired but not imitated, enshrined but not followed, a lonely prophet forever bereft of disciples. For men, he was the shimmering ideal of all they had wanted to be before reality had caught up with them. For women, he offered the strength and loyalty so often lacking in the real men in their lives. In *Pride of the Yankees* there is a very interesting presentation of this myth of the perfect man, when Walter Brennan suspects Cooper of cheating on his wife while he is doing nothing more sinful than teaching some kids to play baseball. As the wife, Teresa Wright plays the scene with a smug complacency that underlines the humor in Brennan's wild assumption. Wright knows that Gary Cooper could never cheat on her, and she is in smiling complicity with the women in the audience, who shared her trust in his virtue.

Almost invariably, Cooper's films deprived him of mystery and menace: two basic ingredients of the movies' successful male sex symbols. Yet his exceptional good looks and his suggestion of repressed eroticism saved him from becoming the shy comic fool, even when given business distressingly akin to a straight-faced Stan Laurel or a male ZaSu Pitts'. In *Good Sam*, when Ann Sheridan hears a crash behind her in church, she does not have to turn around to realize Cooper has dropped the collection box; in *Pride of the Yankees* he

stumbles over a row of baseball bats when he first sees Teresa Wright, who nicknames him "Tanglefoot."

He was always able to rise above this demeaning image of the bumbler and exert an ultra-high frequency attraction that fascinated women. It is a quality that differentiates Cooper from the two other leading "screen innocents" of his era: James Stewart and Henry Fonda. Just imagine the impossibility of either of them tantalizing Dietrich in *Morocco*! Only Cooper could be "nice," even foolish, and yet communicate a secret seductiveness that drew the opposite sex.

This masculine allure was more and more suffused in the aura of sanctity that directors like Frank Capra would later spread around Cooper. But the sex-appeal was dormant, not extinguished: he was in his early forties when he played the circumspect *Dr. Wassell*, yet critic James Agee scored his performance by calling him "a male beauty," and in his late fifties he was still able to sweep Audrey Hepburn literally off her feet in the last shot of *Love in the Afternoon*, when she practically levitates to join him in a final embrace on the platform of a departing train.

There were many sides to Gary Cooper. He was sensual or bashful, adventurous or funny, eminently sane or sublimely crazy. Yet he is best remembered as a hero be-

cause, as Lubitsch once said, the victory of human courage is an irresistible movie theme. Better than any actor, Cooper knew how to suffer stoically on screen, as he was crushed by materialism, cupidity and deceit. He died a thousand spiritual deaths with clenched jaw and furrowed brow, purging the sins of his reverent public.

Thus he survives in movie legend. Coop is the name of the morally torn sheriff Robert Redford plays in *Tell Them Willie Boy Is Here*, and when Cliff Robertson makes a film about an anguished rodeo star, he calls it *J. W. Coop*. Romain Gary's *The Ski Bum*, a novel about the destruction of heroic values, goes under the French title of *Adieu, Gary Cooper*, and when *New York* magazine lamented the disappearance of the American hero, Cooper's color portrait was on the cover, over a mournful plea: "Where are you, Gary Cooper, now that we need you?"

Homages and incarnations multiply as Cooper rides again, a knight in shining armor, on his straight and narrow path to immortality. But there were many detours along the way as he changed routes and shed identities, until he was trapped in the fantasy of millions as the mythical Coop.

Frank Cooper, a lad from Montana, becomes Gary Cooper, sexy silent screen favorite, and then evolves into Coop, elected martyr of the movie-going masses. It is a true story, but so unbelievable that no screenplay would dare try it, even to be played for comedy. In reality, Cooper played it for drama, as his boundaries were lost between the man and the actor, the star and the legend.

On the screen, you could read Gary Cooper like a book. A glint in his eye, a slight contraction of his mouth made dialogue superfluous. Long expository sequences could be bridged with a quickening of his gait or a droop of his shoulders filling the gap and cueing audiences into the character's sudden determination or dejection. In real life, he was not so easy to figure out —people were fooled by his seeming simplicity and then amazed by his underlying complexity.

Gary Cooper was the product of two cultures, melding within him in the tangle of dual personality. The rough, laconic rustic could also be a mild-mannered, almost finicky gentleman. In his television appearances during the late fifties, he astonished viewers who felt somewhat cheated: this wry, elegant man did not act like Coop. He was a living paradox: the Montana cowboy with English breeding.

Frank Cooper was his real name and he was born on May 7, 1901, the second son of British parents who had emigrated to America in the 1880's. His father, Charles Cooper, was a lawyer from Birmingham, England, lured to Montana by his brother's glowing descriptions of silver-lined mountains. The West had by then lost some of its legendary wildness, but it was still unruly enough to energize a righteous,

A LAD FROM MONTANA

taming spirit in Cooper, Sr. He soon forgot the get-rich-quick schemes inspired by the silver boom and went back to practicing his profession, in pursuit of a severe, late Victorian craving for law and order. He became a judge and then rose to a seat on the Montana State Supreme Court.

Cooper's mother was Alice Brazier, a judicious English girl from Kent, equally tempted by her brother's promise of a new life in Helena, Montana. Unsure about her capacity for adapting to this rough, disquieting country, Alice carefully deposited enough money for return fare in a local bank. Once she took a good look at this barely civilized community, she longed to return to the quiet comfort of her native Kent, but the silver boom had gone bust and the bank had frozen her assets. In desperation to get the money and leave Helena, she sought counsel from a lawyer, as reassuringly English as she was. His name was Charles Cooper and when she married him, Alice Brazier gave up her immediate plans—but not her long range aspirations—to return to England.

Her home was in Helena but her heart never deserted Kent. She was repelled by the brawling, sprawling town. Through her prim eyes, it looked nearly savage. The displaced, forlorn wife often pleaded with her husband, but he had turned his back on England and had grown to love the country he was trying to shape into his own ideal of stern justice. The story of the Coopers' marriage reads surprisingly like the plot of a Western, and their marital conflict between inflexible lawman and genteel lady has prophetic overtones of their son's future films, from *The Last Outlaw* and *The Virginian* to *High Noon*.

Confused and uprooted, Alice Cooper existed in a spiritual no man's land and strove to pass this duality onto her children. She did not want Arthur and Frank to grow up as coarse Montana country boys and persuaded her husband to let them receive a British education. She sailed back home with the children and enrolled them in a proper school where they would learn to be proper English gentlemen.

The Cooper boys were looked

With his family on Montana farm. Gary is young boy at left, carrying basket.

down upon as uncouth hayseeds and hazed mercilessly by their English schoolmates, but they soon conformed out of necessity. Their broad Western speech was clipped around the edges into a restrained British accent, their boisterousness toned down by a clamp of Old World reserve. They could have grown up to meet Mama's standards in full, but after two years World War 1 intervened: Arthur and Frank were hurried back to Montana in mid-term.

The process of adaptation was cruelly reversed when they appeared in school at Helena, resplendent in well-cut black suits and Eton collars. Suspicious and hostile toward the youngsters, the local children beat them up, tore the clothes off their backs and sent them home to Mama, half-naked and bruised. Alice Cooper resigned herself to the inevitable and the next day the Cooper children went to school in overalls.

Cooper's adolescence in Helena was hedged by frustration and embarrassment. He was too young to join the Army with his brother Arthur. Denied the adventure of war, he sank into the drudgery of farm work. His father was too involved in the faraway world of politics and only young Frank remained at home, helping his mother run the six-hundred acre farm when nearly every able hand had been drafted.

During the war years, he had to quit his studies and become an expert on all chores, from cow milking to hog calling.

When at last he could return to school, he had grown more than a foot and was taller, thinner and lankier than anybody else in the classroom.

He had travelled between two worlds during his crucial childhood years, suffering alienation and rebuff in both. Now eagerness to please and the fear of rejection came back: he stammered, hung his head, slouched and did everything possible to conceal his conspicuous height and the family breeding that set him apart from the majority. The apologetic stance of *Mr. Deeds* and *John Doe* was already taking shape in his bones.

Cooper had worked well on the farm and his mother had visions of him as a sort of practical Montana variation of the landed gentry she still pined for. Frank was enrolled in Wesleyan Agricultural College but an automobile accident saved him from that fate. His hip was crushed and he again had to drop out of school when a doctor suggested intensive horseback riding as the somewhat unorthodox treatment for his injury.

Painfully he mounted horses hour after hour, perfecting the skill that one day would let him gallop into movies as a stunt man. It was

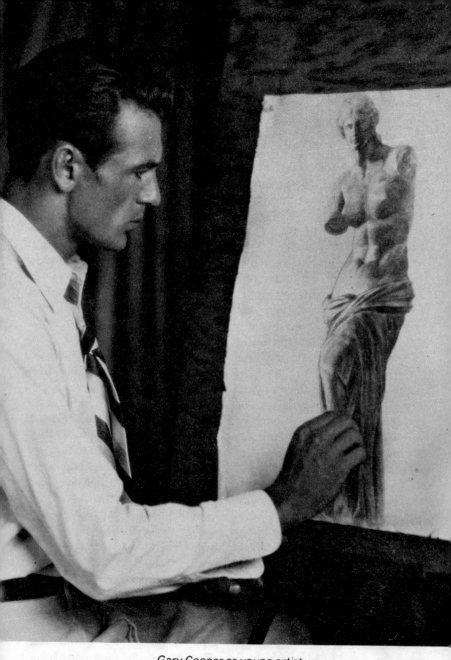

Gary Cooper as young artist.

THE THUNDERING HERD (1925). One of his silent films.

not until he was past forty that X-rays revealed the adolescent Cooper had suffered a fractured hip bone that never healed properly. It turned into a star asset, for he ambled in a rather stiff, asymmetrical pattern that made him identifiable and even expressive when photographed in motion from the back. But with Cooper, every silver lining had its dark cloud and from this broken hip came the racking pains that tormented him during the last twenty years of his life.

He was never a distinguished student. He had little gift for abstraction and books were long rows of words, with no bearing to palpable reality, no challenge to his sharp visual sense. In grim, uninvolved

determination he pleased his folks by going to Grinnell College when he really longed to attend an art school in Chicago. He dared not ask his strict parents for money to indulge in his private ambition to become a political cartoonist.

Cooper was not meant to cross the threshold into his future. Typically, he stumbled into it. Cooper, Sr. had retired from the Montana State Supreme Court and in the early twenties was down in San Diego, California, disentangling the legal end of a complicated family business. Often history repeats itself because family patterns do: just as their families had lured them from England to Montana, the Coopers now began writing glowing letters that would snare their son into joining them in this new land of boundless opportunity.

Young Frank Cooper was not enchanted by the new El Dorado and thought of California as a mere stopover where he could make some money to pay for art schooling in Chicago. West Coast newspapers consistently turned down his naïve cartoons, and he was ready to move on when he met a couple of friends from Montana who were at least paying the weekly bills by working in the budding film industry.

There was great demand for riders in the movie factories that turned out Westerns at the rate of one a week. His friends introduced Cooper as "the best rider in Montana" but the young man's job-hunting outfit was designed to impress editors, not casting directors for action films. He was tagged immediately as a "dude" and his prospective employer seemed less interested in how he rode horses than in how he fell from them. Cooper took off his jacket and ruined his best pair of pants demonstrating that he could bite the dust with the best of them in the battle scenes.

He was hired on the spot and raced through countless Western quickies, rolling down gulches, jumping on and off speeding stagecoaches. It was hard, hellish work, and those condemned to it could only attain purgatory if they managed to get a part with "lines." A title card was the incantation that could turn stunt men and extras into higher paid "actors." Cooper was hunting for "lines" when, after assorted bits in dozens of films, he caught Nan Collins' eye.

Nan Collins was a casting director turned agent and her first idea was to rename her client, against his strong objections. She called him Gary after her home town in Indiana and then unsuccessfully paraded the fledgling cowboy through every front office in town. After numerous turndowns, the newborn Gary Cooper had an insight into what his trouble might be: he was painfully shy and lacked personal magnetism; he should concentrate on trying to sell a screen image. Cooper scraped together sixty-five hard-earned dollars and financed his own test in a Poverty Row studio. He galloped towards the camera, stared at his prospective audience and then fell from the horse.

Again he did the rounds of the studios. The can that contained the single reel of his screen test balanced precariously on his bony, nervously twitching knees as he warmed the bench in the outer offices of diffident producers. There was a glimmer of hope from John Waters, director of many of the Zane Grey Westerns, made at a sub-studio grind factory for cowboy

THE WINNING OF BARBARA WORTH (1926). With Vilma Banky and Ronald Colman.

pictures at Paramount. Cooper was tentatively offered a starring role in *Arizona Bound*, but by then he knew the fickleness of handshake-sealed Hollywood offers. When he heard of a part that required some riding in *The Winning of Barbara Worth* (1926), he ran to the Goldwyn studio, holding his now battered tin can against his chest, like a shield against piercing rejection.

Every major star is a gold mine on which many stake their claim by hindsight. On *The Winning of Barbar Worth*, Cooper has three self-congratulatory prospectors with conflicting versions of his discovery. Samuel Goldwyn has said that he personally informed the aspiring cowboy that the part of Abe Lee had

been cast, but that he kept the rangy amateur in mind and sent for him as soon as Herold Goodwin, delayed by previous commitments, failed to show up on the set.

In her Hollywood memoir *Off With Their Heads*, scenarist Frances Marion tells the same story through different eyes. Goldwyn's secretary had asked Miss Marion to recommend her boyfriend for some movie work. Marion saw Cooper in the waiting room and realized he was ideal for the part of Abe Lee in her *Barbara Worth* screenplay. She won him the role by asking Goldwyn to view the Cooper test in a screening room filled with the company's palpitating female personnel.

THE WINNING OF BARBARA WORTH (1926). As Abe Lee.

Director Henry King is not to be outdone. He claims to have seen Cooper waiting in Goldwyn's office and then to have shown the two-minute screen test to the producer, who merely commented: "Well, it sure proves he can ride." Since the role of Abe Lee was no longer available, King offered Cooper fifty dollars a week to stand by as a cowboy extra. When Herold Goodwin proved absent, King decided to shoot Abe Lee's big scene with Cooper, the better to convince Goldwyn. King smeared the boy's face with dirt, sprinkled him with water to make him look sweaty and had him walk up and down for hours. Cooper was as exhausted as he looked when he ran in front of the camera to warn Ronald Colman that a defective dam was about to burst. "That boy is great!" Goldwyn exclaimed and Cooper became Abe Lee.

Basically, it is really not much of a part: Vilma Banky spurns him in favor of Ronald Colman but the shy young man gets to die nobly in Colman's arms, after averting catastrophe. Banky and Colman were unhappy with the script: their movie star sense told them that the newcomer, if properly trained, could walk away with the picture. The actual shooting was made very difficult for the frightened tyro and, except for director King's faith in him, he would have been sent back from the Utah location.

Henry King had a feeling for backwoods innocence, clearly demonstrated by his phenomenally successful Richard Barthelmess vehicle, Tol'able David. He treated Cooper in the same manner, making him into a radiant figure and turning the picture towards him, just as the stars had feared. The sorrow for Cooper's death was a stronger audience emotion than the elation for Colman's triumph. Cooper's mortal terror of the camera resulted in the kind of withdrawn underplaying that was infrequent in silent films.

Goldwyn realized the newcomer had something, but found him difficult to cast in a studio that did not specialize in Westerns. He hedged a cautious bet by promising Cooper a $65-a-week contract precisely at the point when Paramount made good on its offer to star him in the Zane Grey Westerns. Goldwyn was outbid, let Cooper go, and lived to regret it when he had to hire him at several junctures in his career, at sums the young Cooper never even dreamed of in 1926.

For better or worse, Gary Cooper became a Paramount property. The studio invented him, used him, shaped him. They made him toil, suffer and sweat, in a relentless workout that put muscle into his acting. And to make him soar as a film favorite, they gave him Wings.

In mid-1926, Cooper started out as a Paramount contract player. No stone gathered moss in the studio's quarry. Six of his films were released in the first half of 1927, at the rate of one a month. In John Waters' *Arizona Bound* he had his first cowboy lead as a lad accused of robbery who saves his own skin in five action-packed reels. The true star of the picture was Flash, the Wonder Horse, but Cooper's stunts were duly noted.

He was in two other quickie Westerns. Arthur Rosson's *The Last Outlaw* has Cooper facing his first screen dilemma as a reformed bad boy turned sheriff; he must go after his sweetheart's brother, alienating the girl for a reel or two. In John Waters' *Nevada*, he rescues Thelma Todd from villain William Powell, and the film also rescued him from costarring with the Wonder Horse.

Reviewers remarked that Cooper looked very awkward in his love scene with Todd. Paramount feared the young actor lacked sex-appeal and was only fit to costar with Flash. They need not have worried. Clara Bow, the leading flapper of the movie era, saw him at a studio party and demanded him as costar in her next film.

Cooper was tentatively cast as a playboy in Bow's *Children of Divorce* but there were doubts as to whether the cowboy could make the

ON THE ROAD TO "MOROCCO"

transition so he was given little more than a walk-on as a reporter in Bow's popular flapper comedy, *It*. For Cooper, the film amounted to a screen test in street clothes. He passed it and was immediately set for *Children of Divorce*, an instant disaster.

Twenty-three takes were necessary for his first scene, while he clumsily spilled champagne over a cluster of party girls who surrounded him. He was fired seven times, then rehired for several reasons. For director Frank Lloyd, the taming of Gary Cooper became a matter of pride and he insisted: "I'll make a star out of him if I have to break him." Hedda Hopper, who acted in the picture, concocted a "publicity romance" between the stars, while Clara Bow's intransigent defense of Cooper kept him on the set to the bitter end.

Children of Divorce turned out to be an unreleasable hodge-podge. Josef von Sternberg—who had finished *It* after director Clarence Badger fell ill—was called to do another salvaging job. In his autobiography, *Fun in a Chinese Laundry*, Sternberg says he wanted

28

ARIZONA BOUND (1927).

IT (1927). With William Austin.

CHILDREN OF DIVORCE (1927). With Clara Bow and Esther Ralston.

to scrap the film and start from the beginning, but instead he was given three days to reshoot a third of the script and do the best he could. By then everyone had gone into other cells in the Paramount beehive, so he had to work twenty hours a day over a weekend, with whichever players were available. Cooper was terrified of Sternberg and suffered a case of "Klieg eyes"—an inflammation of his lids—by looking at the potent lights and away from the exacting director.

Sternberg's intervention was less than providential. *Children of Divorce* did not further Cooper's career but the romance with Clara Bow did. He made the rounds of parties and night clubs with the "It" girl and was petrified to find himself tagged as the "It" boy. He disentangled himself from the overpowering Bow and later dismissed the affair as a "a gag." Be that as it may, her influence on his early career is undeniable—she saved him from the Western treadmill. His roles in her vehicles displayed him in front of classier and predominantly feminine audiences. And, thanks to Miss Bow, he landed a tiny but unforgettable role in *Wings* (1927).

It was a remarkable stroke of luck, for in this William A. Wellman World War I drama Cooper is only on the screen for a few minutes. Yet, as in *The Winning of Barbara Worth*, his heroic death made an impact on audiences: it compressed the danger, glory and terror of wartime aviation and sounded like an omen all through the further adventures of the stars, Richard Arlen and Buddy Rogers.

Early in the film, Cooper comes into the trainees' tent, as a flier who fills them with awe. Eager to ingratiate themselves with their future instructor, Rogers and Arlen offer Cadet Cooper a chocolate bar that he barely munches and throws in his bunk. He is the mythical figure: he who must die. Very telling cards are given to his character: he mocks his own valor like a yokel showing off before city folks as he swaggers, "Got to go and do a flock of figure eights before chow." Then he defies augury by snarling, "Luck or no luck, when your times comes you're going to get it."

Minutes after this, Cooper's plane crashes and director Wellman underlines the fatalism by tracking the camera to the half-eaten candy, setting Cooper up as a ghostly presence haunting the film and staying in filmgoers' minds. *Wings* earned Cooper some gratifying notices and was playing to record crowds when Wellman wanted him again for his forthcoming *Legion of the Condemned*, yet had to wait in line for his services. Paramount was by then fully awake to the newcomer's star quality and placed him in *Beau Sabreur* (1928), a follow-up to Ronald

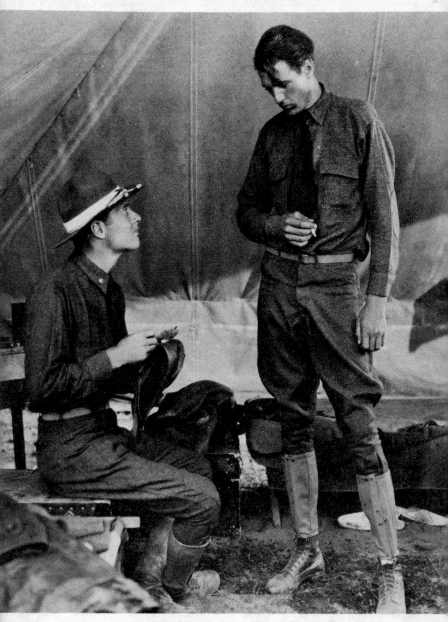

WINGS (1927). With Richard Arlen.

Colman's 1926 version of *Beau Geste*.

Paramount needed Cooper's newborn star charisma to add some class to *Beau Sabreur:* the film was little more than a John Waters-Zane Grey Western in costume, concocted from stock shots and outtakes from *Beau Geste*. Cooper plays a foreign legionnaire with a name that sounds like a bargain wine listing, Henri de Beaujolais. Luckily the picture was silent and he was spared the hazard of playing a Frenchman with a Montana drawl. Magazines fanned the flames of a "romance" with co-star Evelyn Brent, now giving the "It" boy a more appropriate nickname: the "Big Fellow."

After the nonsense of *Beau Sabreur,* Cooper was finally free to come back to director Wellman. *Wings* had capped its box office success by receiving the first Best Film award from the recently created Motion Picture Academy, but parsimonious Paramount did not exactly open the coffers for *Legion of the Condemned* (1928), another out-take film with a threadbare plot strung around aerial photography left over from *Wings*.

In this, the first of their four co-starring films, Cooper and Fay Wray were billed as "Paramount's Glorious Young Lovers." The romance was earthbound but the flying sequences were impressive as Cooper joins a "suicide Squadron"

BEAU SABREUR (1928). With Evelyn Brent.

THE LEGION OF THE CONDEMNED (1928). With Fay Wray.

to forget Wray, whom he mistakenly suspects of being an enemy spy. Wellman took pains to stress the tragic sense of living on borrowed time, and this popular film fired the imagination of many a youngster; Dana Andrews refers to it as the one that decided him to become an actor.

Paramount had started as Famous Players; of all the Hollywood studios it was the one where films were most carefully pivoted around a star's personality. Cooper was now, decidedly, a Famous Player and the front office shrewdly masterminded his career, apportioning the ingredients of his public appeal. In his "man's pictures," the key elements were steely honor, blind courage and flirtation with death. And in his five "woman's pictures" in 1928, a subtle classist element filtered into the plots. The Cooper character fell in love with snobbish girls who initially shunned him and finally succumbed to his manly force.

In Rowland V. Lee's *Doomsday* (1928), Florence Vidor jilts farmer Cooper to marry a rich older man and then, chastened, has the marriage annulled and offers to rehabilitate herself by serving as Cooper's housekeeper for six months. It is clearly love on probation and *Doomsday* is the first statement of a theme that runs through many of Cooper's films for the next three decades—a woman has to earn the right to be worthy of this man.

In *The First Kiss* (1928)—again directed by Rowland V. Lee —Cooper is an impoverished boy of good family. Haughty Fay Wray starts by calling him "white trash" but is finally shamed into admitting his soul is purer than her pedigree. Gregory La Cava's *Half a Bride* (1928) has Cooper as the captain of a yacht owned by socialite Esther Ralston. Her father confines her to the yacht in an effort to stop her marriage to a cad. She escapes in a launch, Cooper jumps overboard to retrieve her and both are marooned on a desert island, where they are forced to essay a "platonic" marriage. *Half a Bride* echoes *Male and Female* and presages *It Happened One Night*, as plebeian Cooper tames the runaway heiress.

Change was added like a spice when the imbalance between lowly Cooper and his highborn ladies was reversed in *Lilac Time* (1928). Colleen Moore is the French waif not fit to marry Cooper, an aristocratic English flier betrothed to an upper-class London girl. Cooper and Moore have an early love-hate relationship that director George Fitzmaurice plays for strained laughs while gamine Moore cavorts all over her country inn with a piledriver cuteness, taking revenge for Cooper's slights by feeding him chicken gizzards and a sandwich smeared with half a jar of mustard.

Then gentleman Cooper stuns Moore by showing her a picture of his mansion. Realizing he has left all that to fight for her beloved France, she drops the hostilities and prays to Joan of Arc, recruiting her patron saint to perform a slightly improper miracle and get Cooper to put his arms around her trembling body.

Cooper was loaned to First National for *Lilac Time*, but the mixture of plot elements followed the Paramount tried-and-true pattern. The shadow of death is again a component of the Cooper formula, and the boys in the suicide squadron are killed one by one, while the survivors bravely down champagne and then smash the glasses in their departed friends' memory. When Cooper's plane crashes, hospital attendants mistakenly report him dead. Moore sends a huge bunch of lilacs to be placed on his body, "as close as possible to his cheek, please." The aroma of the lilacs awakens her wounded lover, who staggers to the hospital window and calls Moore back, just as they are about to be parted forever.

Colleen Moore is touching in this melodramatic coda while Cooper, swathed in bandages and rolling mournful eyes, is quite bad. His quiet and pleasing performance deteriorates in the tear-jerking finale, but this did not mar the subliminal impact of the film. In *Lilac Time* he is again the redeemer of women,

HALF A BRIDE (1928). With Esther Ralston.

LILAC TIME (1928). With Colleen Moore.

raising the poor village girl to his lordly status.

Cooper's candor and steadfastness conquered all. Lost women were brought to him for an object lesson in decency that certified their return to the fold: in Richard Wallace's *The Shopworn Angel* (1928) he is the idealistic World War I soldier who softens a hard-boiled chorus girl (Nancy Carroll). By the time he goes back to die in the trenches, she has absorbed his purity by osmosis and is ready to start a better life in his memory. Another Hollywood innocent, James Stewart, inherited the Cooper part in a much better 1938 remake, with Margaret Sullavan and Walter Pidgeon.

The Shopworn Angel was Cooper's first part-talkie. The sound revolution was sweeping Hollywood and Nancy Carroll sang a couple of hastily added numbers. Cooper only had a chance to say "I do" in their interrupted wedding scene. It did not establish him as a talkie star and, as he later said, "It only proved I could talk."

His full conversion to sound was not achieved by his next movie, either. In *Wolf Song* (1929), the arrangement was similar: Lupe Velez sang musical numbers and Cooper got a few words in edgewise as the fur trapper who kidnaps a fiery señorita, deserts her when the tame life threatens to bore him and —since it was his turn to be

THE SHOPWORN ANGEL (1928). With Nancy Carroll.

chastened—comes back to her at the end.

Director Victor Fleming—who would promote Clark Gable as a ruthless tempter of women—tinged Cooper's proverbial innocence with some bravado and *Wolf Song* first hints at Cooper's sex symbol potential. Rumors circulated about a nude swimming scene with Lupe Velez, but it was not clearly discern-

ible when finally shown in long shot. Undoubtedly, it was the presence of Miss Velez that loosened Cooper's strait-laced image. For two years they had a tempestuous love affair.

Paramount strongly objected to the liaison and there were veiled threats of front office punishment if they dared to get married. Until he met Velez, Cooper—though

WOLF SONG (1929). With Lupe Velez.

BETRAYAL (1929). With Esther Ralston.

THE VIRGINIAN (1929). With Walter Huston.

twenty-seven years old and a full-fledged star—still dutifully lived at home with his parents. The studio disapproved of all the publicity about Velez' and Cooper's wild fights and passionate reconciliations, but Paramount staff writers were encouraged to add a pinch of wickedness to a personality so simon pure that it was in danger of becoming Simple Simon.

In Cooper's last silent film, *Betrayal* (1929), he is a curly-haired and moody artist who covets the girl he left behind (Esther Ralston), now married to old Emil Jannings. The film sounded the death knell for Jannings' career in Hollywood. In a new, more realistic film world on the verge of sound, there was little place for heavy emoting. Cooper self-effacingly refused to be drawn into the plot's melodramatic vortex, but Jannings gladly jumped into it and sank. *Betrayal*, made as a talkie, was released minus a soundtrack where Jannings' English was unintelligible and his bellowing intolerable.

George Cukor told Gavin Lambert a revealing anecdote about the disparity in Cooper's and Jannings' styles. Fighting exhaustion in Paramount's film factory atmosphere, Cooper had developed the ability to fall asleep quite soundly between takes. In *Betrayal*, director Lewis Milestone shot sixty feet of Cooper sleeping, then woke him up suddenly and printed the take for further use in the picture. When Milestone showed Jannings the scene, the grand old actor was truly shaken and gasped: "That young man should play Hamlet!"

Fortunately he never did, but he was immediately starred in *The Virginian* (1929), his first all-talking picture and a landmark in his career. It was the third of several remakes of Owen Wister's novel, an ever-resilient classic that finally ballooned and burst as an empty, endless television serial in the sixties. The ingredients were still fresh when Cooper wore the rigid ethos of the hero like a tight holster around his narrow hips.

Director Victor Fleming, with the psychological insight of a born star-maker, trimmed away all the genteel, fey and whimsical aspects in Cooper's personality, which were later used to great advantage in memorable comedies. What Fleming needed for *The Virginian* was the unilateral hardness, the masculine singleness of purpose currently rebaptized as *machismo*.

Cooper plays the uncompromising lawman not above hanging his best friend (Richard Arlen) who is dealing with cattle rustlers. *The Virginian* does what he must, following a code so limited between the black and the white, the positive and the negative, that he taciturnly veers from "Yup" to "Nope," with

ONLY THE BRAVE (1930). With Mary Brian.

no gray "Maybes" in between. In the film's most memorable scene he is confronted in a saloon by the villain, Trampas (Walter Huston). As the bad man murmurs something very much like "son of a bitch," Cooper caresses his revolver and in a tone so calm that it falls neatly between the amused and the menacing, warns Trampas: "If you want to call me that, smile."

. *The Virginian* portends *High Noon* in the loneliness of the hero's quest and in his clash of standards with a sentimental girlfriend (Mary Brian), who turns away from Cooper after he sends Arlen to the gallows. They reconcile and it is precisely on their wedding day that

The Virginian must face Trampas for the decisive shoot-out. He does his job, just as Marshal Will Kane would, twenty-five years later, not in venom but with regret for the violence forced upon him by evil circumstance.

Fleming underlined the inherent bluster in Gable, making him a world favorite, but he had the tact to let Cooper play *The Virginian* quietly, introvertedly, almost tragically. Henry Hathaway was on the set as assistant director, a job he had previously held in *Wolf Song* and *The Shopworn Angel:* he was watching Cooper like a hawk and making mental notes for the day when he would get his hands on the actor and

SEVEN DAYS LEAVE (1930). As Kenneth Dowey.

guide him through seven films.

Hathaway had to bide his time for several years while Cooper made films like Frank Tuttle's *Only the Brave* (1930), an inconsequential Civil War drama that critics called a setback to his career. Cooper also lent his name as one of the many contract players in *Paramount on Parade* (1930). His musical sequence was photographed in color and showed his light blue eyes to devastating effect among the ladies. The studio's mail department chalked up a 40% increase in the fan mail he was getting from love-struck females.

Cooper actually believed that Paramount was doing him a favor when they cast him in *Seven Days Leave* (1930), an unabashed tear-jerker based on J.M. Barrie's *The Old Lady Shows her Medals*, with Beryl Mercer repeating her Broadway success as the charlady who pretends to be a war hero's mother. After mildly chiding her for her deception, Cooper "adopts" her and she gets the medals when he is killed in action.

Director Richard Wallace made sure that buckets of tears were shed as he peeled this glossy movie onion, but Cooper put a firm clutch on the sentiment. He waded through this sob fest with remarkable restraint, like a distant relative at a raucous Irish wake.

Paramount liked *Seven Days Leave* and held up its release, presumably to cash in on the sentiment by making it a Christmas attraction.

Convinced that the combination of Cooper with little old ladies would prove unbeatable, the studio rushed him into John Cromwell's *The Texan* (1930), as a con man bent on fleecing sweet Emma Dunn by posing as her long lost son, then undergoing a change of heart under the influence of the dowager's pretty niece (Fay Wray).

Cooper was physically depleted by the strain of hopscotching from one film to the next and he dozed constantly on the set. Studio personnel called him "Sleeping Beauty" behind his back and Hathaway—again Cromwell's assistant in *The Texan*—escorted one of the scoffers to a recumbent Cooper. Waking him with a start, he told him: "We're shooting a scene right now where you have to look at this man." Even half asleep, Cooper reacted fast before adjusting his expression and asked: "Do I like this man or not?" Hathaway roared in triumph to the miscreant: "You see, he's a thinking actor."

There was little to think about in *The Texan*, though, and Cooper was entirely justified for dozing through it. *Seven Days Leave* also failed to live up to expectations and Cooper was consigned to another World War I melodrama, Rowland V. Lee's *A Man from Wyoming* (1930), in which he is mistakenly reported dead in action but comes back to redeem June Collyer, who has taken to wild partying to ease the pain of widowhood. The critics had grown tired of Cooper's periodic resurrections and rightly called the film "preposterous."

Cooper fared much better with *The Spoilers* (1930), the third of five remakes of the Rex Beach novel. The picture was well received and its main attraction was—as in all film adaptations of the book—a smashing saloon brawl between Cooper and William Boyd, effectively staged by director Edwin Carewe. The rest, with Cooper preferring honest Kay Johnson to conniving Betty Compson, is tepid and dull, with none of the excitement Marlene Dietrich would bring to the 1942 version, co-starring John Wayne and Randolph Scott.

In his first six 1930 movies, Cooper was in a rut. He was close to being taken for granted. In the abstract marriage of star and public it is often necessary to dispel the monotony with a change of pace, a touch of mystery. Cooper was to be endowed with new magic by the unlikeliest of sorcerers when Josef von Sternberg refurbished him as a fascinating sex symbol in *Morocco* (1930).

The film had been chosen to present Marlene Dietrich to American audiences. *The Blue Angel* had not yet opened in the United States and Sternberg's instincts as an entrepreneur told him that the heartless Lola Lola could make a deleterious first impression. In *Morocco*, Sternberg reversed *The Blue Angel*, making Dietrich the obsessed lover and Cooper the unattainable, disdainful man who drives her into self-immolating frenzy. Cooper was an odd choice to embody the allure of the eternal male, but Sternberg disregarded his previous image and set the stage so brilliantly that his character's attraction is not only believable but irresistible.

The director had studied the Russian film masters and had the subliminal powers of montage at the tip of his fingers. He employs them marvelously in Cooper's entrance into *Morocco*, intercutting between his arrival as a conquering Foreign Legionnaire and the women who vie for his favors. A flighty whore deceives her pimp by giving Cooper a seductive glance and a Muslim woman lifts her veils to offer him the naked secret of her beauty, in rash defiance of sense and tradition. Each shot is minimally held on the screen, with the camera always returning to Cooper's face, in a spiralling crescendo of sexual invitation.

When Cooper first sees Dietrich singing in a cabaret, both know they have met their match and size each other up like gladiators entering a sensual arena. She tauntingly hands

THE SPOILERS (1930). With Betty Compson.

MOROCCO (1930). With Marlene Dietrich.

him a rose and he mocks the offering by placing the flower behind his ear, like a clerk would a pencil or a hood a cigarette. Hostilities are openly declared between them and from then on they pursue or rebuff each other in the passionate abandon of a dance of desire where male and female alternately lead or follow.

Their mercurial status as master and slave changes constantly. Dietrich gets the upper hand when she persuades Cooper to desert the Legion. While he waits in her dressing room, he fingers the jewels a rich admirer has given Dietrich and then puts on her top hat. Gazing into the mirror, he realizes what he is about to become, grabs her lipstick and on the glistening surface writes: "I'm sorry, I've changed my mind."

Enraged by the flight of the man she thought vanquished, Dietrich smashes a champagne glass against the mocking mirror and proceeds to exert her wiles on the next available male, Adolphe Menjou. His offer of riches and respectability is no compensation for her visceral loss, and Dietrich gets her comeuppance in

MOROCCO (1930). With Marlene Dietrich.

an extraordinary sequence in which drums herald the return of the downtrodden Legionnaires, interrupting the engagement party Menjou has organized for her.

The drums call Dietrich to Cooper and she must follow blindly. She clutches the pearl necklace Menjou had given her and breaks it, symbolically destroying her relationship to a man she is not interested in torturing. Dietrich has lost the sadomasochistic game that runs through *Morocco:* she would rather be Cooper's slave than Menjou's mistress. Madly, she trails her Legionnaire lover into the desert like an Arab camp follower, discarding her high heels as the last token of her previous existence, stumbling along in the sand on her way to probable doom.

Sternberg had altered the pattern of Cooper roles from apostle of redemption to Pied Piper of damnation. The director knew he could bring out Cooper's charisma in the cutting room, through a jigsaw puzzle of erotic editing. He left him alone on the set while he conferred in German with the nervous Dietrich. Cooper felt he was being deliberately ignored and he yawned audibly during one of the hushed exchanges between the female star and her mentor, provoking Sternberg into walking off in a pique.

Cooper felt something peculiar was going on and he was right. Sternberg treated his actors as objects and Cooper was being classified as a phallic symbol. All through the film he is as inscrutable and mesmerizing as the idol Greta Garbo dances around in *Mata Hari.* Cooper does not perform in *Morocco*—he is performed against. It must have been a blow to his budding actor's ego, but it was a powerful shot in the arm for his star image. *Morocco* was the box office success that rescued Paramount from bankruptcy and Cooper from goody-goody dullness. Yet he resented the film as an invasion of his privacy, a shedding of a carefully pinned seventh veil.

Cooper liked working with Dietrich, but risked suspension by turning down a co-starring role in *Dishonored.* He refused to work with von Sternberg. The Svengali-like director had shown a side of Cooper's personality that he would rather keep hidden. He had been led astray on the road to *Morocco,* but he would never again make a movie like this one.

Summing up his career, Cooper once said: "I want to do stories that are credible, that fit my personality and don't clash with people's beliefs about me." As early as 1930, he felt *Morocco* did not fit this scheme and he welcomed going back to a Western, a film genre he would always revert to as a tranquilizer during troubled periods of his life.

After a whiff of Sternberg's rarefied atmosphere, *Fighting Caravans* (1931) gave him plenty of breathing space. The film was a harbinger of the Cecil B. DeMille outdoor extravaganzas Cooper would breeze through in the coming decade. It boasted of two directors (Otto Brower and David Burton), two photographers and a top-heavy production staff, all engaged in costly location work.

Fighting Caravans, planned as a super-production, was ill-timed. According to 1931 box office receipts, Westerns were down and gangster films were up, so Paramount gave Cooper his only brush with this genre in Rouben Mamoulian's *City Streets*. The director persuaded Dashiell Hammett to put some muscle into a flabby two-page synopsis, vaguely based on Clara Bow's silent *Ladies of the Mob*. Hammett, a fine crime novelist in his own right, prepared a screen treatment which was later tampered with and was finally attributed to Oliver H.P. Garrett and Max Marcin.

WAITING FOR "MR. DEEDS"

Beset by personal scandal and terrified by sound, Clara Bow withdrew from the film at the last moment and Cooper costarred with newcomer Sylvia Sidney. Acting for dear life to make a strong impression, Sidney added some substance to the crudely motivated part of the mobster's daughter who lures her "straight" boyfriend into the beer racket. She then has second thoughts while serving a term in the women's penitentiary and comes back to get Cooper out of the claws of the mob.

Mamoulian eluded the plot's inconsistencies by staging the film in a half-world of light and shadow, so unrealistic that anything could have happened in its nightmarish confines. He turned *City Streets* into an exercise in style, with pioneer use of sound for the heroine's interior monologue, and also into a triumph of legerdemain, with ten cleverly suggested off-screen killings.

Cooper's performance ambiguously charts the young man's slow intoxication with the glamour of the underworld. He bats his eyelids as if

FIGHTING CARAVANS (1931). With Lily Damita.

he were literally blinded with pride as he demonstrates he can shoot his own handkerchief in mid-air. And Sylvia Sidney's half-tough, half-plangent heroine provided the right chemistry for a very effective, but unfortunately never repeated, screen coupling.

City Streets was shot mostly at night, because Cooper was working in another film in the daytime. He was making $750 a week and no tears can be shed over the plight of a highly salaried actor in the midst of the Depression, but nonetheless his working conditions at Paramount were on the sweat-shop level. Mamoulian remembers that during a fifteen-hour shooting schedule over a weekend, Cooper and Sidney fell asleep in the middle of an amorous close-up.

Marion Gering's *I Take This Woman* (1931)—made back-to-back with *City Streets*—was still another variation of the rich girl-simple man conflict. Carole Lombard displays her special brand of acidity as the heiress who marries a cowboy on her father's ranch, mainly to spite the old buzzard who sent her down there to atone for a prank. Cooper plays it straight and the contrast between styles adds a dash of piquancy to a flavorless film.

The romance with Lupe Velez was over and Cooper was depressed and weary. He staggered through *City Streets* and *I Take This Woman* and then collapsed. Doctors diag-

CITY STREETS (1931). With Sylvia Sidney.

nosed a combination of anemia and jaundice. Paramount grudgingly granted him a leave of absence. The studio was instantly on the alert when, instead of checking into a hospital, Cooper headed for a much needed vacation in Venice. He had a strong constitution and recovered quickly in the company of Countess di Frasso, née Dorothy Taylor, a New York heiress who had briefly married into the Italian nobility.

Dorothy di Frasso can be credited with the final polishing of Gary Cooper. She took him to an expensive tailor for two dozen dapper suits, introduced him to royalty and café society and picked the last

of the hayseed from his hair. Paramount read all this in the gossip columns and summoned Cooper back to start on Edward Sloman's *His Woman* (1931).

In this trifle he was a tramp steamer captain who adopts a foundling, advertises for a governess to take care of the child and hires Claudette Colbert, a dancer fleeing involvement in a blackmail case. They are separated by inane plot complications but the baby's illness brings them back together. Naturally, the child survives. The movie didn't. And Cooper barely made it.

His symptoms returned during the hectic shooting and he fell into a

I TAKE THIS WOMAN (1931). With Carole Lombard.

HIS WOMAN (1931). As Captain Sam Whalan.

DEVIL AND THE DEEP (1932). With Charles Laughton and Tallulah Bankhead.

hepatitis stupor, rolled in a blanket in a corner of the set. He had lost twenty pounds and was all sallow skin and puncturing bones. Colbert almost could not sit on his lap for a love scene and pleaded with the studio to cancel the picture and send Cooper to the hospital. He had strength enough to make it to the last day of shooting, but when the ordeal was over he threw all caution to the winds and sailed on an extended vacation that included a hunting safari in Africa, with Countess di Frasso at his elbow.

"A guy who can shoot rhinoceros can shoot a movie," a Hollywood columnist quipped. Paramount decided it was time to scare their errant star with a menacing replacement. They picked Archie Leach, an English chap rebaptized Cary Grant, a name so similar to Gary Cooper that the message would be easy to get. Grant began making the pictures scheduled for Cooper, including *Madame Butterfly* and *Hot Saturday.* Cooper rushed back, flanked by the Countess, to face this upstart the studio had cast as his nemesis.

Both actors were in Marion Gering's *Devil and the Deep* (1932), in which Charles Laughton re-

IF I HAD A MILLION (1932). With Jack Oakie and Roscoe Karns.

hearsed for his future Captain Bligh in *Mutiny on the Bounty* by playing a sadistic submarine commander. The object of his justified jealous tantrums is Tallulah Bankhead, the unfaithful wife who first dallies with Grant, then with Cooper.

Devil and the Deep is one of the funniest disasters in screen history and the ineffable climax—where Bankhead escapes the sunken sub by floating up thirty feet of water in a black chiffon gown—is "camp" elevated to surrealism. Oddly enough, the film restored Cooper's self-confidence—he was proud to be playing against recognized stage

luminaries like Laughton and Bankhead—and felt he had nothing to fear from Cary Grant, whom he shrewdly assessed as "a crack comedian, no competition for me."

Fortified with some solid business advice from the astute Countess, Cooper was able to bluff his way through a confrontation with Paramount's high echelon. They did not know that Cooper's bargaining position was quite weak, since his European capers had left him almost broke. The haggling was successful and he signed a seven-year contract, starting at $2,500 a week with options escalating to

$7,500 a week. There was also a promise of better pictures, beginning with *A Farewell to Arms*, Frank Borzage's screen version of Hemingway's best seller.

Before the new contract was in effect, Paramount extracted every drop out of the old arrangement and Cooper completed one of the weaker sketches in *If I Had a Million* (1932), as a soldier who gives away the fortune implied in the title, thinking it is part of an April Fool's gag. Norman McLeod directed his stint and then guided Cooper in the later released *Alice in Wonderland* (1933), a delightful and unjustly neglected fantasy in which Cooper masquerades as the White Knight, equipped with bulbous nose, scraggly white mane, bald pate, and clanking armor.

A Farewell to Arms (1933) was a sugar-coated version of Hemingway's novel. The main themes of illicit wartime love and military desertion were glossed over as the lovers perform a do-it-yourself

A FAREWELL TO ARMS (1932). With Adolphe Menjou, Mary Phillips, and Helen Hayes.

ceremony by murmuring their vows in church, with rather distant benefit of clergy. Cooper can then run away to Switzerland, not to live in sin with his mistress but to anxiously rush to his pseudo-wife's death bed. Two final scenes were shot, with Helen Hayes alternately dying or surviving. The happy ending was chosen, to Hemingway's annoyance, but when the film was re-released in 1948 audiences could finally see Miss Hayes expire, to the strains of Wagner's *Liebestod* from *Tristan and Isolde*.

No matter how they ended, the characters had ceased to belong to Hemingway and had become Frank Borzage's. They thrived in this gifted director's sealed-in universe.

Cooper's naturalism and Hayes' theatricality do not clash but coexist in the film's dreamlike cocoon. Even today, the film preserves the faint, evanescent aura of a long forgotten sachet, left in the bottom of a seldom opened cedar chest. In 1933 its power was undiminished and it became a box office and critical success. The Academy nominated it as best film, and it received awards for its photography and sound recording.

In *A Farewell to Arms*, Borzage had artfully managed to turn a masculine novel into a woman's picture. A similar, but unsuccessful conversion was attempted in Cooper's next film, *Today We Live* (1933). He was loaned to MGM for this movie ver-

TODAY WE LIVE (1933). With Roscoe Karns and Robert Young.

sion of a William Faulkner story called "Turnabout." In its original form, it was a World War I drama with no women in the cast and a deep concentration on the male camaraderie that has always been director Howard Hawks' forte.

Hawks was delighted with the screenplay he had commissioned from Faulkner, but then MGM needed an urgent Joan Crawford vehicle and Hawks asked the author to make over one of the characters into a Crawford heroine. Faulkner worked for five days on the sex change but he must have failed at the operation because two adapters, Edith Fitzgerald and Dwight Taylor, were given added credits for the script. In its final form, the film has sacrificial Crawford giving up Cooper to marry Robert Young, a childhood sweetheart blinded in combat. Cooper then signs for one of his customary suicide missions while Young, refusing Crawford's pity, plots with Franchot Tone to be sent on the same deadly errand. Tone is unfortunately late in disentangling all the conflicting sacrifices and both Cooper and Young die while running in this nobility sweepstakes.

Hawks tried to disregard the soap operatics but to this day he regrets Crawford's intervention in his all-male drama. Hawks told *Cahiers du Cinema* that she had made matters worse by trying to talk like one of the boys. The film, though fatally maimed, still has some good war scenes plus the virile hard core Hawks aimed for and even soulful Miss Crawford could not crack completely. *Today We Live* is a negligible film for Cooper the actor, but it was significant for Cooper, the man. Sandra Shaw, an aspiring actress, had a later cut bit part in it, but she was to play a major role in the Gary Cooper story.

Sandra Shaw was the name chosen by Veronica Balfe, a strikingly beautiful East Coast socialite trying to break into the movies with the help of her uncle, MGM's powerful set designer Cedric Gibbons. Cooper met Veronica, nicknamed Rocky, at one of Gibbons' sumptuous parties; very soon the Countess di Frasso went into eclipse. Life imitated art as Cooper found himself in a true version of his frequent scenarios about the stubborn cowboy and the unattainable heiress.

Rocky's family objected to her marrying an actor with a reputed penchant for high living and Cooper spent almost a year in the winning of Veronica Balfe. He did not have much time to brood over the troubled courtship because his Paramount schedule was as heavy as ever and he was being given the stronger roles demanded in his new contract.

In *One Sunday Afternoon* (1933), he was a bitter dentist who felt he

With wife Rocky.

had married the wrong girl and wondered what his life would have been with his true love (Fay Wray). The film was based on a popular play by Frank Hagan and was remade twice in the forties as Raoul Walsh's *Strawberry Blonde* with James Cagney, Olivia de Havilland and Rita Hayworth, and then under its original title as a musical with Dennis Morgan, Janis Paige and Dorothy Malone. The thirties' picture, directed by Stephen Roberts, is no match for the Walsh version, but Cooper gives a quiet pathos to the role of a man torn between illusion and reality; it opened a new acting range for him.

His range was still limited and he went beyond it in *Design for Living*

(1933). The brittle Noel Coward play revolved around a *menage à trois* and director Ernst Lubitsch feared he could not get away with all the sexual innuendo and sophisticated dialogue in a mass-oriented movie. The screenplay was entrusted to Ben Hecht, who not merely rewrote but actively dismantled the Coward original. Lubitsch had sensibly wanted to discard all except the title, but Hecht tried to keep the central situation intact while eliminating all but one of Coward's lines, a toast "to the good of our immortal souls" during Cooper's very funny drunken scene.

Lubitsch was not very happy with the hybrid script but the starting

ONE SUNDAY AFTERNOON (1933). With Fay Wray, Neil Hamilton, and Frances Fuller.

DESIGN FOR LIVING (1933). With Miriam Hopkins.

date was imminent and he cast Miriam Hopkins as the woman, with Fredric March and Douglas Fairbanks, Jr. as the men who share her more or less platonically. When Fairbanks, Jr. was hospitalized with pneumonia, Cooper was sent in as a last-minute replacement. He was justifiably wary of a part Coward had written and acted with his own brand of supercilious finesse. The Ben Hecht character was more accessible to Cooper, but he is still a little incongruous as a lionized portrait painter in Paris: there is much nervous hand wringing through the saucy repartee.

Lubitsch did everything possible to put Cooper at ease—he praised his acting constantly and goaded him to play with the authority of a star. *Design for Living* was Cooper's first outright comedy and Lubitsch was enchanted with his innate flair, although star and director must have sensed he was miscast in high comedy, however dutifully Hecht had lowered it for the general public.

Lubitsch proclaimed Cooper the most photogenic of performers and said he was "like wax you could mold in front of a camera." He insisted that, as the most malleable and sensible of the *Design for Living* star trio, Cooper had saved the picture. Not quite but almost, for Cooper is directly responsible for the film's best remembered scene, when for the first time a streak of

OPERATOR 13. (1933). With Marion Davies.

comic madness flickers in his eyes as he hilariously prepares to break up a party thrown by snobbish Edward Everett Horton.

Operator 13, Cooper's last 1933 release, was a Marion Davies vehicle for which he was lent to Cosmopolitan-MGM. Cooper plays a Confederate soldier and Davies is a Yankee spy who invades the South disguised as an octoroon laundress. William Randolph Hearst directed a couple of scenes in this film, after Richard Boleslavsky threw in the megaphone, unable to persuade Hearst to let Davies play for low comedy instead of high-flown romance. *Operator 13* falls between both genres, into the no man's land now labelled as "camp."

Offscreen, Cooper had better luck. In real life, as in his movies, love conquered all. Convinced that Cooper had sown the last of his wild oats, Rocky Balfe's parents gave the bride away on December 15, 1933. Sandra Shaw quashed all her dreams of stardom and entered into an equally scintillating career as Rocky Cooper, one of the most refined and respected *grandes dames* in Hollywood circles.

Cooper's private life was taking its definitive shape and soon his screen image would follow suit. After waiting for seven years, Henry Hathaway finally got a crack at directing him. *Now and Forever* (1934), a Shirley Temple picture, seemed an inauspicious start for the fruitful Cooper-Hathaway tandem. In the wake of Temple's upsurge, her appearances were less films than rituals, cinematic Adorations of the Magi with the golden-haired moppet smiling benedictions all around her. Yet, within this constricting framework, Hathaway was able to extract a fine performance from Cooper, and many were outraged when he failed to receive an Academy Award nomination for it.

Cooper has a shady, almost Gable-like role as the questionable con man who plans to sell his little daughter to a wealthy relative bent on bringing up baby in a stuffy milieu. Even wisecracking Carole Lombard, as the woman in Cooper's life, is repelled by the scheme. Of course, Temple wins her father's heart in the long run, and he redeems himself with a remarkable lack of cheap sentimentality.

Now and Forever, disregarded as a minor Cooper film, is really a curious experiment, with director Hathaway trying to find out how far the star's charisma could be stretched without snapping. The film created a storm of protest among Temple fans, and when Fox finally handled her career their writers were careful never again to place Miss Curly Top in such disreputable company. After negative reactions at a sneak preview, the movie was further tampered with

NOW AND FOREVER (1934). With Carole Lombard, Shirley Temple, and Andre Charon.

and a happier ending devised as Cooper and Lombard leave Temple, safely adopted by a rich benefactress.

Gone was the original climax in which the tarnished lovers died in a car crash, with Cooper paying in full for his initial callousness. Even without the final punishment, the scramble with sin and retribution did not pass unnoticed and *The New York Sun*, reviewing *Now and Forever*, mentioned Cooper's "commendable dignity in martyrdom, since after his reformation he is crushed by every misfortune."

Another atypical role awaited Cooper at the Goldwyn studio. The producer who had let him escape ten years before now dearly paid for his services. Cooper's star dust was supposed to brush off on Anna Sten, a European import Goldwyn had tried desperately to impose on the public. Sten possessed beauty and possibly talent but Goldwyn had remade her, à la Frankenstein, from spare parts of Dietrich and Garbo. The result, though by no means monstrous, was definitely not marketable.

The Wedding Night (1935) was conceived as Sten's do-or-die film and Goldwyn himself stood behind the cameras coaxing the stars with one of his oft-quoted malapropisms: "If this isn't the goddamned greatest love scene, this picture will go right up out of the sewer." Perhaps inspired by all

THE WEDDING NIGHT (1935). With Anna Sten.

THE WEDDING NIGHT (1935). With Anna Sten.

this frantic pep talk, director King Vidor tried to stop Cooper from mumbling words and stumbling over lines, to no avail. "Imagine my amazement"—Vidor later confessed—"when on the screen I observed and heard a performance that overflowed with charm and personality. I learned an indelible lesson."

The Wedding Night is quite advanced for its time. Cooper plays a jaded and blocked New York writer, forced by bankruptcy to return to his Connecticut farm. His bored wife (Helen Vinson) runs back to the city and Cooper's loneliness is dispelled by close contact with a nearby community of tobacco growing Polish immigrants. His link with their primitive, apparently idyllic world is Manya (Anna Sten), who mocks Cooper's laziness and alienation, prodding him to write a book as simply as she milks her cow.

Shamed into hard work, Cooper writes four chapters of a novel about his newly found Utopia. Manya recognizes herself as the protagonist, Sonya, and the film takes a Pirandellian turn as the real girl and the fictional character intermingle, with Manya either giving clues or taking hints from the Sonya she reads about every night in the writer's kitchen.

Vidor's film overturns the back to nature mystique as Cooper discovers he cannot separate the adorable quaintness of these people from their pettiness and imbecility. Visiting Manya's family, he savors a deliciously exotic prune soup with the adults while he angrily notices the children waiting on a bench, ready to pounce ravenously on the leftovers, as soon as their elders have gorged themselves. This is a prelude to his horror in seeing Manya sold into marital slavery by her greedy father.

The screenplay reties the Pirandellian knot when Cooper's wife returns from her Park Avenue haunts and reads her husband's manuscript. In a well written confrontation scene, she tells Manya that their meeting in the novel is unconvincing, for the real wife would never surrender her husband to the Polish girl. Manya-Sonya accepts the verdict and marries her father's choice, Fredrik (Ralph Bellamy). On their wedding night, Fredrik doubts her virginity and in a drunken rage runs out to kill Cooper. Trying to warn him, Manya falls down a flight of stairs to her death.

The Wedding Night can now be appreciated as an interesting period piece, but in 1935 it was doomed. In the urban confinement of Depression America there was a longing for the lost paradise of country life. Vidor's obstinate, contrary film, rubbed audiences the wrong way and flopped resoundingly. Anna Sten carried the blame and

THE LIVES OF A BENGAL LANCER (1935). As Captain McGregor, disguised as an Afridi tribesman.

Goldwyn gave up on her. Cooper returned to Paramount, where Henry Hathaway had a tailor-made vehicle waiting for him: *The Lives of a Bengal Lancer* (1935).

Hathaway had been working on this picture for years. On an expedition to India he had shot miles of film for an aborted Ernest Schoedsack project and had all the material at hand for the right story and the right performer. He counted on Cooper to unify his efforts and not a seam was visible when Hathaway welded the documentary footage with superbly lit Paramount sets. In its mixture of courage and mayhem, loyalty and bravado, *The Lives of a Bengal Lancer* is a boy's fantasy come to life.

Hathaway again cast Cooper in a Gable-like role. As Captain McGregor he sports a thin mustache and a rebellious attitude from the first line, when he curses the Colonel's orders, to the last, when he dies blasting the military bugle. McGregor defies authority and is often reprimanded for disobeying stupid orders. His individualism wins over a new recruit (Franchot Tone), who strives to become his buddy, but Tone's wit and sophistication make Cooper uneasy.

In this masculine world, friendship and loyalty are pillars of team spirit. Tone is hurt when Cooper's preference centers on Richard Cromwell, the baby-faced son of a stick-in-the-mud Colonel (Sir Guy Standing). Rejected by a father terrified by shows of favoritism, Cromwell is "adopted" by Cooper, and a tense all-male triangle develops when Tone starts taunting Cooper for his protectiveness to the young boy. "It comes out in all of us, the mother instinct," Tone quips, a needle in every word. And from then on he jokingly calls Cooper "Mother McGregor."

Cooper characters were often mistrustful of females and *The Lives of a Bengal Lancer* is the first of his films where a sullen, misogynistic tone creeps into the screenplay. Little by little, the three men form a sturdy alliance that is eventually threatened by a woman. Inexperienced Cromwell takes the bait and is seduced by Mohammed Khan's favorite (Kathleen Burke). The Khan (Douglas Dumbrille) is seized with murderous jealousy and swears revenge.

Allied to save the unwitting Cromwell, Cooper and Tone fall into a trap and are brutally tortured. Both men forget their initial animosity and seal a pact of mutual respect in a dungeon, while sharing a cigarette held by trembling, charred fingers. Hathaway lets all the tensions blow sky-high in a whirlwind action finale, as British troops storm the Khan's fortress and Cooper dies heroically. The Academy ignored Cooper's perfor-

PETER IBBETSON (1935). With Ann Harding.

mance but *The Lives of a Bengal Lancer* was up for the best film award and Hathaway received the only Oscar nomination in his long and underrated career.

Hathaway was determined to establish Cooper as an actor of breadth and versatility. Both men went out on a limb in their boldest experiment, the ultra-romantic *Peter Ibbetson* (1935), based on the George DuMaurier novel that had been a stage hit in 1917, with Constance Collier costarring opposite John and Lionel Barrymore. George Fitzmaurice had previously filmed it in 1922 as *Forever,* with Wallace Reid, but Paramount felt the story could now reach its full poetic bloom as a talking picture.

Peter Ibbetson contains some of the best and worst acting of Cooper's first decade as a movie star. Presaging *The Fountainhead* by thirteen years, he is cast as an individualistic London architect who refuses to build any structure unworthy of his artistic vision. His spiritual malaise stems from the memory of a lost childhood sweetheart and, on a Parisian journey to recapture his past, he reenters the garden of his tender years. Cooper achieves a feat of economic acting as his mental recollection materializes the invisible girl with no tricky superimpositions—he faces the camera, eyes lit from within, lips curved in a smile of recognition, and convincingly whispers "Hello" into the void.

Back in England, architect Cooper is commissioned to rebuild the stables of the Duke of Tower's manor. He is startled to discover the Duchess (Ann Harding) is the very same girl he once loved. Cooper is again excellent as he admits his love in the presence of the husband, (John Halliday), who stands between the pair, watching in disbelief, obliterated by the intensity of the lovers' passion.

On the verge of abducting the Duchess, Cooper accidentally kills Halliday and spends the rest of his life in a dungeon, but the woman senses a bond so strong that they can meet in their dreams, back in the glistening garden of their childhood. It is here that the screenplay needs an actor like John Barrymore, whose rich voice and precise diction could infuse pedestrian lines with an illusion of poetry. Cooper's performance is rent down the middle—awkward with the florid language but infinitely moving as his face silently expresses rage, impotence and unbearable love, growing older every day in prison and younger every night in the private dream world he shares with the faraway Duchess.

Peter Ibbetson is as uneven as Cooper's performance, but it still casts a spell while the lovers have either idyllic trysts or catastrophic nightmares that look mysteriously like the good or bad LSD trips so prominently featured in the sixties drug culture movies. This wondrously imaginative, incurably romantic film has developed a cult and is fondly remembered while far more integrated pictures have faded into oblivion.

Cooper's malleability made him a prize acquisition and many directors at Paramount were bidding for his services. As the studio's production chief for a brief time in 1936, Ernst Lubitsch could pull rank, and he secured Cooper to costar with Marlene Dietrich in *Desire*. His newly acquired responsibilities as top man prevented Lubitsch from actually directing the picture and Frank Borzage received a somewhat disputed credit for it. Lubitsch was constantly on the set and had mapped the film so exactly that many feel Borzage functioned as conductor to Lubitsch's composition and orchestration.

In *Desire*, Dietrich is a thief who drops a necklace in Cooper's pocket to get past suspicious officials on the Franco-Spanish border. She then tags her unwitting accomplice to retrieve the jewel. In the six-year span since *Morocco*, the stars' roles had been completely reversed: Dietrich is the irresistible force and Cooper the highly moveable object. Despite its steamy title, *Desire* is far from the dark von Sternberg world:

DESIRE (1936). With Marlene Dietrich.

it is a glowing Lubitsch comedy where every sexy glare is interrupted by a knowing wink.

The temptress is not all bad and her prey is not all that innocent. There is detachment and irony in Cooper's performance; he may be Dietrich's foil but he's nobody's fool. *Morocco* was a battle of the sexes but *Desire* is a droll skirmish between sparring partners who find out that love may be pain, but also a lot of fun.

After the giddy pleasures of *Desire*, Cooper was due for a jolt. In Paramount's world of fantasy and adventure, his characters had been blissfully preserved from the harsh realities of the Depression. (Mamoulian's *City Streets* is such an anomalous exception that it hardly serves even to prove the rule.) Cooper had to go to Columbia to face the bleak thirties in Frank Capra's *Mr. Deeds Goes to Town* (1936).

It was not a square but an oblique confrontation with reality, for it took place in the fairy tale America of Capra's populist fantasies. With his uncanny talent as an image maker, Capra envisioned Cooper as a contemporary folk hero and turned him into Mr. Deeds, champion of the depressed poor, who plants the seeds of mild revolution in the lush gardens of the filthy rich.

Longfellow Deeds is a small town man who gets by on the slim profits of a small business and writes greet-

MR. DEEDS GOES TO TOWN (1936). On the set with director Frank Capra.

MR. DEEDS GOES TO TOWN (1936). With Jean Arthur.

ing card doggerel on the side. He also plays the tuba and shows an amiable quaintness that places him on that safe shore of madness called eccentricity. When Deeds inherits twenty million dollars and goes to town, he becomes the victim of greedy con men and opportunists. Journalists prey upon his antics to entertain their fun-starved readers—Deeds is turned into a living joke.

An unscrupulous "news hen" (Jean Arthur) wheedles herself into his confidence and invents a catchy tag for him, "The Cinderella Man." She pretends to share his country boy delight as he feeds doughnuts to a horse and rides the fireman's wagon, while photographers for her daily paper follow at a safe distance and use Deeds' childlike escapades as fodder for the front page trough.

Capra does not allow his characters to cavort carelessly beyond a few reels; soon both Cooper and Arthur face "reality," with almost simultaneous crises of conscience. Arthur's cynicism crumbles when he dedicates a lame but touching poem to her. Cooper's unconcern is shattered when a destitute farmer, crazed by reading about Deeds' senseless capers, tries to shoot him and bursts into tears instead.

A socially conscious Deeds plans to apportion his millions to give the downtrodden a share of the wealth. Capitalists declare war on Deeds, led by a vanguard of "shyster" lawyers. A hearing is rigged to declare him insane. Realizing the girl he loves took part in the conspiracy against him, Deeds refuses to defend himself, sinks into stony silence and is about to be committed when proof of Jean Arthur's devotion makes him snap back. He takes his own defense in a riotous scene in which he demonstrates that one and all, including the judge, are every bit as "crazy" as he is.

Audiences loved him through the film and then idolized him in the classic worm-turning conclusion, when he becomes an American Quixote tilting at Establishment windmills in a seizure of Midwestern madness that Robert Riskin's screenplay glorifies as "pixilation." Depression audiences cheered Deeds and shared vicariously in his hour of victory, as he defeats his cunning and amoral enemies with the anti-intellectual weapon of plain common sense.

Mr. Deeds Goes to Town was selected by the New York critics as the best film of 1936, won the Academy Award and garnered a second Oscar for Capra. Cooper received his first nomination but lost to Paul Muni's *Louis Pasteur,* a mannered performance that looked more like *acting* at the time. It did not matter in the end, because Cooper's Deeds had gone beyond mere characterization into popular mythology.

Capra had refused to make *Mr. Deeds* with any other actor, realizing that only Cooper could bear the burden he had placed on his shoulders. His impact on movie-goers carried beyond the film, and in the public eye Cooper became a screen apostle of valor, a patron of decency, a talisman against despair. From then on, the audience had the last word. No matter what Cooper did, no matter what he played, by his Deeds they would know him.

Hollywood of the thirties moved at breakneck speed and often the studios had no time to reevaluate their most profitable star properties. Even after the significant shift of gears in *Mr. Deeds*, the Cooper image at Paramount moved forward on past momentum. Most of his late thirties films failed to develop the quiet, homespun courage Capra had illuminated. The Cooper hero was still woven into flashier, wider, adventurous tapestries.

Lewis Milestone's *The General Died at Dawn* (1936) set this pace with Cooper as O'Hara, the upright American who smuggles gold to help the cause of Chinese peasants against a brutal warlord. Clifford Odets' screenplay tried to recycle a pulp novel into political melodrama, but most of his social overtones went under, like raisins in a fluffy cake. After many revisions of the original, it would be unkind to blame Odets for scenes such as the one in which Cooper tells Madeleine Carroll: "We could have made beautiful music together."

Cooper plays a cut-and-dried hero: his motives are bluntly stated from the first scene, when a crass bystander watches the shackled peasants on their way to debtor's prison and justifies the tyrant's edict because the men had failed to pay their taxes. Cooper asks the loud-

OF SAINTS AND SINNERS

mouth for a match, the man excuses himself for not having any and Cooper abruptly punches him, pointing out that lack of money and lack of matches are the same: the blow and the imprisonment are equally brutal and unjustified.

As O'Hara, Cooper is once more betrayed by a woman (Madeleine Carroll), the unwilling cohort of a dishonest father (Porter Hall). Cooper enlightens the shady lady, but they are both captured by evil General Chang (Akim Tamiroff). In the climax, Chang has his men kill each other and then, before expiring himself, he lets Cooper and Carroll escape, after O'Hara's promise to gain him immortality by telling the world about his reign of terror. *The General Died at Dawn* is outrageous fantasy, held in rein by Cooper's discretion and Lewis Milestone's visual panache. It is easy to dismiss it as an overblown comic strip, but difficult to resist its fascination.

Cooper then walked surefootedly into legend with *The Plainsman* (1936), playing the first of his real-heroes, Wild Bill Hickok. Cecil B. DeMille demanded granite-like

THE GENERAL DIED AT DAWN (1936). With J.M. Kerrigan, Dudley Digges, and Madeleine Carroll.

protagonists for his movie friezes and dependable Cooper gave Hickok the exact epic thrust. There is no tongue-tied hesitancy, no bumbling self-consciousness in his remarkably assured performance: he can petrify cheaters at a glance during a poker game, and when he says: "You're not leaving town unless dead men can walk," it is less a threat than a statement of inalterable fact.

Cooper's *Plainsman* is fearless with men but apprehensive with women. He is courteously awed by Louisa Cody (Helen Burgess), the ladylike wife of his friend Buffalo Bill (James Ellison). He feels more at ease with Calamity Jane (Jean Arthur), a leathery frontier virago who drives a stage coach and whiplashes her enemies at the slightest provocation. The Cooper misogyny is most evident when he repels Calamity's romantic advances and brushes the back of his hand over his lips after she kisses him: "You're not wiping it off," Calamity jeers, "you're rubbing it in."

"Women and me don't agree" is his often repeated maxim. Yet Calamity is on the verge of conquering his mistrust when she falls under the influence of Buffalo Bill's wife. Mrs. Cody gives her a lovely dress, a coquettish hat, and soon Calamity lives up to her name. All this finery has softened her, the screenplay suggests: Cooper is unflinching when the Indians torture him, but Calamity can't stand the sight of his suffering and reveals the position of the Cavalry.

Cooper holds her responsible for the ensuing massacre and never forgives her. Shot in the back by a coward (Porter Hall), he expires on a barroom floor and only in death can Calamity possess him. She brushes her lips against his now cold mouth and whispers: "This is one kiss you won't be able to wipe off." The film ends poetically with Cooper's body melting into a shot of wavering wheat stalks that fade into a group of galloping riders in a vivid film metaphor: the dead hero is like the grain from which a race of giants will germinate.

Cooper's screen persona was by then so purged of ambiguity that Henry Hathaway dared to cast him in a dangerous role as a man accused of multiple homicide in *Souls at Sea* (1937). After a shipwreck, Cooper beats and then shoots the frenzied men who are about to capsize a rescue boat overloaded with women and children. He has taken life to preserve life and the agonizing choice has left him drained and dazed. Just like Longfellow Deeds, he sits stolidly in court, refusing to defend himself. He works his mouth in a mixture of gnawing guilt and injured pride, hearing himself berated as a murderer. Even Frances Dee, as the woman he loves, has typically deserted the Cooper

character and is the first to point an accusing finger at him.

As always, Hathaway sets an appropriate framework for Cooper. For contrast, there is the sidekick, Powdah (George Raft), who looks for cheap girls in every port while Cooper dedicates himself to lofty abolitionist ideals. Both men undergo torture side by side, just as Cooper and Franchot Tone did in *The Lives of a Bengal Lancer,* but this time it is Cooper who breaks down to protect his friend, just as Jean Arthur had in *The Plainsman*.

This sharing of pain intensifies the bond between the men. Cooper goes around quoting from *Hamlet* while Raft plays the noble brute, turning the first third of the film into a seafaring *Of Mice and Men*. Cooper feels a brotherly responsibility toward his shipmate, but is so wary of his tenderness that he cautiously crosses out the word "Dear" in a note he addresses to Powdah.

Virginal Cooper has been keeping himself pure for the right girl and when he meets Frances Dee, Hathaway gives him a captivating bit of pantomime to express his hidden feelings: Cooper steals a rose from Dee, puts it in a vase, looks adoringly at it and even takes his hat off to the flower. It is typical of the careful detail Hathaway embroidered in Cooper's performances, especially after the director caught

THE PLAINSMAN (1936). Porter Hall and Jean Arthur confront the fatally shot Cooper.

SOULS AT SEA (1937). With George Raft.

on to the Capra trick of making Cooper lovable and laughable at the same time. *Souls at Sea* abounds in this mingling of romance and humor, climaxed by the moment when Cooper is trying to woo the girl and ends up with the hiccups.

His well-shaded, sweet and sour performance failed to have the desired impact because *Souls at Sea*, planned as a roadshow presentation, was shorn of a third of its footage and released with no particular fanfare. Designed as an Oscar-winning blockbuster, it only received nominations for its score and interior decoration. Hal Walker, Hathaway's assistant director, was also nominated in this later dropped category, a clear indication that the film's special effects were considered more effective than its drama of conscience.

Cooper was consoled from this disappointment by the birth of Maria, the daughter he would love

SOULS AT SEA (1937). With Frances Dee.

THE ADVENTURES OF MARCO POLO (1938). With Basil Rathbone.

above all else, but there are hints that Paramount's shabby treatment of *Souls at Sea* had something to do with his signing with Samuel Goldwyn when his home studio was inexplicably late in picking up his option. Incensed at being caught napping, Paramount took the matter to court. For the next two years, until the end of his obligation to Paramount, Cooper shuttled between the two studios.

Cooper's first Goldwyn film under the new arrangement was *The Adventures of Marco Polo* (1938). Director John Cromwell quit the film after a week, allegedly baffled by the irreverent tone of

Robert E. Sherwood's screenplay. Archie Mayo finished the picture and its reception by audiences and critics remains a mystery: *Marco Polo* is evidently intended as a spoof and one wonders why everyone was so embarrassed when reviewers accused it of provoking "involuntary laughs."

No straightforward adventure film would have George Barbier as a delightfully improbable Kublai Khan, or Alan Hale and Binnie Barnes playing the Barbarian chief and his wife as the Mongolian equivalents of Jiggs and Maggie. Cooper, shifty-eyed and tongue-in-cheek, is a joy to watch, but the film's surreptitious humor eluded everyone and *Marco Polo* did not travel far in the area of box office receipts.

Cooper was staging a quiet rebellion at Paramount and he gave the studio a hard time by refusing Kipling's *The Light That Failed* as too gloomy. It was made, gloomily indeed, by William A. Wellman with Ronald Colman, after Cooper's Paramount contract ran out. Instead, he went gladly into *Bluebeard's Eighth Wife* (1938), but this time Lubitsch's sunny world was overcast by a perverse Charles Brackett-Billy Wilder script.

In this acidulous screwball comedy, Claudette Colbert discovers, just before the wedding, that millionaire Cooper has had seven previous wives. She marries him in spite, just to get a juicy divorce settlement, and the labyrinthine plot revolves around Colbert's devices to keep her husband from consummating the marriage. They are seen in Venice, crossing in the night on separate gondolas, and in Prague, where Cooper cools his ardor and fights insomnia by spelling Czechoslovakia backwards.

When the bitter honeymoon is over, Colbert taunts Cooper by insinuating an affair with a mystified David Niven. She munches scallions to avoid being kissed by the increasingly frenetic husband. The film careens into black comedy in an ugly finale: Cooper, thoroughly

BLUEBEARD'S EIGHTH WIFE (1938). With Claudette Colbert and Rolfe Sedan.

THE COWBOY AND THE LADY (1938). With Walter Brennan and Fuzzy Knight.

unhinged by abstinence and frustration, is rescued from an insane asylum by Colbert. Their fade-out embrace is only possible after he snaps out of a strait-jacket.

Lubitsch's sense of humor could not leaven the underlying nastiness of *Bluebeard's Eighth Wife*. Despite its undeniable high spots, the film communicates an uneasiness that turns guffaws into groans. Thirties' audiences could not believe that Cooper had actually married and divorced all those women, and secretly hoped that some trick of mistaken identity would resolve the ending. When this last minute vindication of Cooper did not materialize, the film was given the cold shoulder usually reserved for nasty gossips who go around spreading incredible rumors about a nice guy.

Cooper returned to Goldwyn for *The Cowboy and the Lady* (1938), a throwback to the classist romances of his early silent pictures. Merle Oberon, daughter of a presidential candidate and future First Young Lady of the land, is sent down to Palm Beach after she's been caught dancing in a gambling house with her octogenarian uncle (Harry Davenport). Bored to death in Florida, she goes on a blind date with her maid (Patsy Kelly) and meets Cooper, a rodeo cowboy.

She pretends to be a lady's maid who supports her dad and four younger sisters. Cooper immediately honors her by calling her "the work horse that carries the load," and brands her employer as a worthless "show horse." Oberon cannot reveal she is really the "show horse" and tries to disillusion Cooper by pretending to be a flirt. He proceeds to dump her in the pool and, since no thirties' film heiress was immune to such treatment, Oberon amorously pursues him to the Galveston rodeo.

On the boat to Galveston, he is placed in a sexy situation in her cabin, but after a heated embrace he promptly swallows his Adam's apple and runs to wake up the ship's captain, insisting that "Where I come from, when a man feels about a girl like I do, they get married." After the wedding, Oberon is summoned back to help her father's political campaign. Cooper follows her, crashes the elegant dinner she is hosting and is laughed at by shallow plutocrats. He lets them have it in *Mr. Deeds* fashion and even Oberon's ambitious father, shamed by the cowboy's lesson in practical democracy, gives up presidential aspirations to share pancakes on his son-in-law's ranch.

The inside story on why this awful film was made is a classic example of how helpless stars were sent in to pitch with the bases loaded after the producer had thrown the game. Leo McCarey had written the original story in three days, to pay for hospital bills. William Wyler helped him sell it by telling Samuel Goldwyn that he liked it. The favor completed, Wyler backed out. When Goldwyn offered McCarey a chance to direct his own story, McCarey declined, saying frankly that he would not "touch that crap." Goldwyn threw good money after bad by hiring S. N. Behrman and Sonya Levien to patch up the irreparable. H.C. Potter finished *The Cowboy and the Lady* and, needless to say, the critics really roasted this old chestnut.

With three flops in a row, Cooper needed a hit. He surprised many when he backed away from playing Rhett Butler in *Gone With The Wind*, a part he judged too rascally and sexy for his special talents. He preferred to be the valiant *Beau Geste* (1939), a foreign legionnaire who battles Arabs and a sadistic commander (Brian Donlevy). He is finally deified as a Viking hero by brother Robert Preston, who lights his funeral pyre and then carries the Norse ritual to perfection by placing the villainous "dog" (Donlevy) at Cooper's feet.

As it turned out, the "dog" got the lion's share of the praise and Donlevy received an Academy Award nomination for his supporting role. William A. Wellman's lustrous production and punchy direction made *Beau Geste* into the big success Cooper required at this point, for

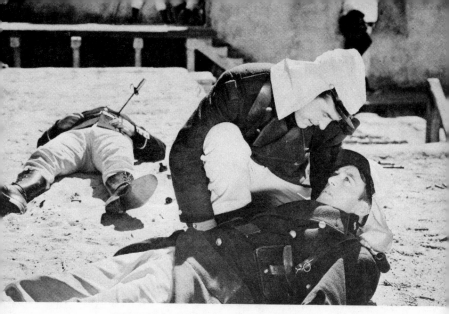

BEAU GESTE (1939). With Ray Milland.

the film was his last under his Paramount contract and he had decided to freelance as soon as his obligation to Goldwyn ran out.

At Cooper's request, Goldwyn hired Henry Hathaway to guide him through *The Real Glory* (1939), a rousing action film structured along the lines of *The Lives of a Bengal Lancer:* the masculine trio is back in action, this time with David Niven and Broderick Crawford as soldiers of fortune who join forces with Cooper, an American doctor in the Philippines, shortly after the Spanish-American war. They aim to quash a Moro uprising that threatens to wipe out the whole garrison. Though not as strongly as in the early film, the women (Andrea Leeds and Kay Johnson) are again cause for dissension and magnets for danger.

As in *The Lives of a Bengal Lancer,* Cooper plays an individualist who dislikes following orders and is placed under arrest for trying his own methods of fighting the Moros by capitalizing on their religious fanaticism: he menaces the natives with eternal damnation by announcing every dead rebel will be buried inside a pig's skin. The film is easily the goriest and most violent in Cooper's career, especially in a breathless last sequence when the Moros attack with catapults, a dam is blown up and Cooper destroys the villain, perfidious Alipang (Tetsu Komai).

THE REAL GLORY (1939). With Broderick Crawford and David Niven.

THE WESTERNER (1940). With Walter Brennan.

Hathaway fantasies of adolescent *machismo* had reached their apex with *The Real Glory* and Cooper wanted something deeper, more sensitive. Unlike most stars of his era, Cooper was very mindful of who would direct him, and yearned to work with William Wyler. Yet when Goldwyn offered him the next Wyler project, Cooper was discouraged. One look at the screenplay of *The Westerner* (1940) was enough to convince him that he would merely be providing star assistance to Walter Brennan, who indisputably had the central role as the fabled Judge Roy Bean.

Wyler gave Cooper a "There are no small parts, only small actors" kind of sermon and he was shamed into accepting *The Westerner*. Having twisted his arm, Wyler directed Cooper with great sympathy and gave him some good scenes, such as the one in which he realizes Brennan's obsession with famed singer Lily Langtry and escapes the hangman's noose literally by a hair: he convinces Brennan that he personally knows Miss Langtry and can get him one of her precious locks in exchange for his life.

Aside from these bright snippets of characterization, Cooper does not have much to do until *The Westerner's* superb climax: Brennan has bought an entire house to be a one-man audience at Lily Langtry's Texas debut, but as the curtain rises there is only Cooper, standing in the center of the stage and primed for dead reckoning. This indelible moment now seems the only claim to the film's unwarranted reputation.

The Westerner is, in fact, a slow and self-consciously "arty" film, with cinematographer Gregg Toland straining for poetry in static compositions fraught with gnarled trees and cottony clouds. Walter Brennan won his third supporting Oscar for his excellent portrayal of the hanging Judge, and also sabotaged what little tension the picture had, for his Roy Bean is so mischievously appealing that Cooper—and the audience—are plunged into dramatic indecision as to whether he should be shot or spanked.

Cecil B. DeMille needed an epic actor for *North West Mounted Police* (1940) and Paramount had to meet Cooper's terms. It was the first Technicolor feature for both Cooper and DeMille: the director imaginatively used the process to emphasize how Cooper, a Texas ranger, stands in awe of the red splendor of the Mounties' uniforms. *The Plainsman*, one of DeMille's simpler and finer films, had relied on Cooper's backbone to keep the story erect, but in *North West Mounted Police* the director was playing with a brand new kaleidoscope and the visuals have it over the dramatics.

NORTH WEST MOUNTED POLICE (1940). With Madeleine Carroll.

MEET JOHN DOE (1941). With Edward Arnold and Barbara Stanwyck.

Whether confronting Indian chief Big Bear (Walter Hampden) or engaging in a mild romance with a frontier nurse (Madeleine Carroll), Cooper is limited to do his archetypal best. As often happened in DeMille's gaudiest melodramas, the bad people became as colorful as the decor and the scenery, leaving not even the spoils for the virtuous. *North West Mounted Police* is stolen by Paulette Goddard and Robert Preston, who stage a very animated teeth-gnashing tournament as a half-breed wench and a treacherous Mountie.

Not one of Cooper's eleven films since *Mr. Deeds Goes to Town* had even remotely approached its quality. Frank Capra again came to the rescue with *Meet John Doe* (1941). As Long John Willoughby, Cooper plays a down-and-out baseball pitcher recruited to enact one of those human interest charades in which thirties and forties journalism turned yellow at the edges. He is to impersonate John Doe, a man so defeated by the poverty and meanness of the world that he publicly announces his intention of jumping off the highest building on Christmas Eve.

Cooper's heartless manipulator is once more a newspaperwoman (Barbara Stanwyck), who invented the bogus story as a venomous parting shot at the paper that had cancelled her "sob sister" column. When the accidentally published

89

"John Doe suicide note" creates a stir, she is rehired and forced to cast somebody as her fictional correspondent. She pronounces Long John perfect for the part. He is, in fact, so perfect that people start believing his message of altruistic wisdom and soon the whole scheme has mushroomed into a national movement to band all the John Does of America together under a "Love Thy Neighbor" banner.

John is drawn into living a lie he has now come to accept as truth. Gradually, he realizes that the good he can do is forever compromised by the evil that spawned it. Tycoon Edward Arnold blackmails him into fronting a plan to turn the populist movement into a Fascist conspiracy: Long John has no option but to tell the truth that will personally discredit him as John Doe.

Cooper's performance runs the gamut from initial amusement to growing involvement, regret, bewilderment and ultimate despair, as he faces a mocking crowd that jeers and pelts him with rotten fruit and vindictive scorn. Anger and pity fluctuate in his wounded-animal eyes, but he forgives his tormentors for they know not what they do. His face is drenched in rain and tears as he leaves the chaotic rally, on the way to an inevitable Gethsemane from which the film abruptly and fatally detours him.

Capra had come to the moment of truth but could not face it. Four endings were shot and discarded for *Meet John Doe*. In his autobiography, Capra reveals how, in desperation, he consulted an able script doctor, Jules Furthman, famous for finding solutions to troubled films by equating them with standard plots, from Shakespeare to the Bible. Astonishingly, Furthman told Capra and his scenarist Robert Riskin that their story had no possible conclusion because they did not have a story in the first place.

Maybe Furthman did not include the New Testament among his sources for script ideas, because *Meet John Doe* is really a forties parable about a Messianic figure who can only prove his true nature as savior by embracing death. Long John Willoughby had reached a dead end and the only logical and dramatic alternative was to fulfill his promise to jump off the roof and be posthumously recognized by the faithful as the true John Doe.

In the fifth and official ending, Capra drives his rebuked prophet to the verge of immolation and then backtracks. A few of the loyal disciples appear on the roof at the last moment, accompanied by Stanwyck, the sobbingly repentant Magdalene. Instead of killing himself, John leaves with his apostles while James Gleason, a pugnacious Peter the Fisherman, confronts

MEET JOHN DOE (1941). With Barbara Stanwyck.

Pharisee Edward Arnold with the cockeyed optimism of his last line clincher: "There's the people! See if you can lick that!"

This forcedly optimistic conclusion compromised *Meet John Doe* and the film was not given its due as a flawed masterpiece. After all the soul-searching ordeal with the five endings, Cooper was as turned off by Capra's "saints" as he had been by von Sternberg's sinners. He was looking around for a relaxing Western when he was literally drafted into playing *Sergeant York* (1941).

Goldwyn had decided to lend Cooper to Warners for this picture, in exchange for Bette Davis, his chosen star for *The Little Foxes*. Cooper objected to the maneuver but was soon persuaded by a coalition of men and arguments. Alvin C. York, the World War I hero, would allow only Cooper to impersonate him. Director Howard Hawks reminded Cooper that producer Jesse L. Lasky had given him his first chance to be a star at Paramount, and now needed his cooperation to launch this pet project at Warners. Last, but not least, it seemed inevitable that America would go to war against Nazi Germany and it was strongly argued that Cooper had a patriotic duty to lend himself to this recruiting poster of a film.

Cooper visited Alvin York on his Tennessee farm and a long conversation with the hero finally swayed him into tackling this arduous role. In *Sergeant York,* Cooper goes through a triple conversion: he is at first a hell-raiser, in splendid scenes that Hawks brings to the verge of hillbilly comedy, especially in Cooper's relationship with his mother, played with stony perfection by Margaret Wycherly. He reforms out of love for Joan Leslie and labors to buy a plot of bottom land to settle on with his future bride. Tricked into losing both the option and his money, he flies into a murderous rage but is stopped when a bolt of lightning hits his rifle.

York interprets this as a miracle and gets religion with a vengeance. Even his fiancée loses her patience at his dogged passivity and forbearance. When war is declared against Germany, York registers as a conscientious objector: he feels he has no right to take a man's life, even if the man is classified as the enemy. *Sergeant York* then takes on an added dimension and it is immediately clear why Cooper was essential to the project: only he could bring off the film's last third.

Recruited against his will, York procrastinates in battle until he sees his buddy "Pusher" (George Tobias) killed by German bullets. He exercises an unspoken providential mandate to take arms against the Huns by declaring: "I had to stop those guns from killing all those

SERGEANT YORK (1941). With Joan Leslie and June Lockhart.

SERGEANT YORK (1941). With Stanley Ridges and Harvey Stephens.

men." These scenes are not developed as a call to violence, but almost as a childlike prank. When Cooper gobbles like a turkey, a curious German raises his head and he promptly shoots him. From then on, Cooper wipes out thirty-five machine gunners and takes 132 prisoners in the Argonne forest. Yet he is not presented as the Avenging Angel called into Holy War, but as Peck's Bad Boy, Tom Sawyer and Li'l Abner all rolled into one.

The film's war sequences are very ambiguous when compared with Lewis Milestone's treatment of death in the trenches in *All Quiet on the Western Front:* these are not soulful German youths trying to catch butterflies, but human ciphers in a shooting gallery, with disquieting echoes of the turkey shoot York wins early in the movie. Crude and unfeeling though this conclusion now seems, *Sergeant York* has to be placed in proper historical perspective as a film conceived in fear and anger as Hitler's armies overran Europe.

The Cooper character had failed against the homegrown Fascism represented by Edward Arnold in *Meet John Doe,* but now America was in imminent trouble and there was no time for losers. Cooper's performance insinuated that it was possible to win by countering the enemy's brutality, yet remain pure and boyish at heart. Part hagiography, part battle cry, *Sergeant York* helped set the mood for the impending sacrifice that was to be demanded of America's youth.

Within these very narrow limits, Cooper's performance is surprisingly varied, as he grades the different shadings of fanaticism that impel York to the absolute extremes of godlessness and piety, pacifism and violence. In a blaze of patriotism right after Pearl Harbor, Cooper was chosen best actor of the year by the New York Film Critics and then received an Academy Award which he dedicated to York, "the one who really deserves this honor."

Sergeant York made Cooper an idol. His age and his hip injury prevented him from enlisting to fight Nazism, but he tirelessly went on war bond rallies and army camp tours, covering 23,000 miles and entertaining soldiers all over fighting fronts in the Pacific. At home and abroad, he embodied all the virtues of the good American: conscientious and honest, freedom-loving and family-minded.

Even the scoffers had acknowledged him as one of the most proficient screen actors in Hollywood and he was way up on the list of box office champions. It was his golden hour: he was on top of the world—with nowhere to go but down.

SERGEANT YORK (1941). York and the captured German troops.

Cooper was coming into hard times, personally and professionally, but he had no hint of this in 1941, when he thoroughly enjoyed himself with *Ball of Fire*, the comedy Goldwyn had promised him after *Sergeant York*. "Once upon a time in New York," reads the opening title card of this sassy fairy tale in which the Charles Brackett-Billy Wilder screenplay cynically upturns *Snow White and the Seven Dwarfs*.

Barbara Stanwyck plays Sugarpuss O'Shea, a brash night club singer fleeing a subpoena that might force her to incriminate her gangster lover (Dana Andrews). She takes refuge in the home of seven musty professors deep in research for an encyclopedia. The eighth and much younger scholar is Professor Potts (Gary Cooper), a philologist assigned to write the entry on slang: his enthusiasm is boundless as he dips into Sugarpuss' reservoir of newly minted terms. The wicked Snow White defeats the witchlike housekeeper and then seduces the seven old codgers by teaching them to dance the conga, but her sights are set on Cooper, the flesh-and-blood mixture of Bashful and Prince Charming.

In his comedies, director Howard Hawks loved to invert the sexes for piquant effect and in *Ball of Fire* Stanwyck is the tough guy and

GOOD TIMES/ BAD TIMES

Cooper the shy maiden. He retreats and she advances, reassuring him that it is all in the name of science by leering: "Remember the guy who learned a lot from a falling apple? Well, think of me as an apple." She needs Cooper's protection to evade the police and is relentless in her attack. After giving him a preview of coming attractions by letting him feel her wet foot, Sugarpuss smells surrender in the air when he confesses he had to splash water on the back of his neck after seeing the sunlight shining through her hair. "You're a regular yum-yum, you drive me wacky," she purrs as she piles books to stand on, the better to reach him for a conquering kiss.

Sugarpuss has Professor Potts on a string she doesn't really want to pull, until Brackett and Wilder come up with a scene that delineates Cooper's image as the inexperienced but ardent male. In a man-to-man talk with Richard Haydn—the only professor who is a widower—Cooper anxiously admits he may not be able to follow Haydn's advice about a hands-off honeymoon with Sugarpuss, because his rampaging desire threatens to get the best of him.

BALL OF FIRE (1941). With Barbara Stanwyck and the seven professors.

That is all Sugarpuss needs to hear, for Cooper has mistakenly entered her dark bedroom and addressed his confession not to the starchy professor but to the suddenly excited bride-to-be. Hawks focuses on Stanwyck's greedy eyes gleaming in the shadows before she passionately pounces on Cooper, sensing that all his careful repression is about to explode spectacularly.

The encounter is interrupted by Dana Andrews, the gangster lover, who abducts the reluctant Sugarpuss. She will have nothing to do with him and still pines for Cooper, whose odd sex appeal she defines between fond sighs: "Oh, he can get drunk on buttermilk, blushes up to his ears and doesn't even know how to kiss, the jerk." Finally Cooper rescues her and, boxing manual in hand, makes mincemeat out of Andrews.

Ball of Fire, one of the best and least touted of screwball comedies, combines the verbal pyrotechnics and diamond hardness of the Brackett-Wilder team with the wise and mellow humanism of director Hawks. The film throws away valuable character actors with the abandon of a millionaire lighting cigars with hundred dollar bills: there are cheerful bits by Oscar Homolka, S.Z. Sakall, Allen Jenkins, Henry Travers, Dan Duryea, Leonid Kinskey, Tully Marshall, Aubrey Mather and Elisha Cook.

Cooper wanted to top *Ball of Fire* with another comedy, but Goldwyn had indulged him enough and now, duly impressed by *Sergeant York*, the producer wanted to probe further into his star's folk hero potential. In *Pride of the Yankees* (1942), Cooper plays Lou Gehrig, the revered baseball pitcher who had died of muscular distrophy at the age of thirty-eight.

The Herman J. Mankiewicz-Jo Swerling screenplay is wishful thinking on a mass scale: Gehrig is fashioned into a true proletarian paragon who realizes every immigrant dream of rising to fame from obscure beginnings. Gehrig's German Mama is a cook at a Columbia University fraternity and she hopes Lou will soar far above his father's janitor status to become an engineer like her brother Otto. Gehrig reluctantly goes along with her fantasy, playing baseball all day and cramming down detested books at night.

When Mama falls seriously ill, Gehrig pays the steep hospital bills by signing as a rookie with the Yankees. As soon as he becomes a baseball star, Mama turns into his Number One fan and, dazzled by his glory on the pitcher's mound, she defiantly exclaims: "The world is full of engineers but how many Lou Gehrigs are there?"

In *Pride of the Yankees* Cooper enacts a full catalogue of fantasies: you need no schooling to get to the top; you can teach your know-all

PRIDE OF THE YANKEES (1942). With Walter Brennan.

parents a practical lesson; you can have an eternally happy and faithful marriage and, at the end, you can even achieve immortality in the love of those you leave behind. Cooper walked through this American dream world with the conviction of Everyman as seen by Norman Rockwell.

He gives an outstanding performance and, in the last half hour, he touches greatness. Cooper makes Gehrig's physical disintegration doubly terrifying by playing it without a trace of self-pity. Not a muscle flutters in his poker face, but his eyes seethe with rage and hurt as the fickle crowd boos his errors in the park. Later, in the locker room, he tries to tie his shoelaces with half-paralyzed fingers and falls on the floor, looking around for any witnesses to his humiliation.

The film challenges Cooper's capacity for understatement and also his oddball sense of humor. He brings off an impossible scene where he is made to discuss Gehrig's terminal illness in sports terms, and poignantly asks the doctor whether he has three strikes against him. There is such dignity in his acting that even the built-in pathos of Gehrig's farewell speech rings fresh, true and unrehearsed. When this stricken man faces 62,000 fans in the stadium and says: "Today I consider myself the luckiest man on the face of the earth," one of the screen's unforgettable moments is right up there in close-up.

Pride of the Yankees broke a long-time jinx and was one of the very few baseball pictures to succeed at the box office. It received eight Academy Award nominations, including a third one for Cooper, who lost to James Cagney in *Yankee Doodle Dandy*. Cooper had enjoyed working with director Sam Wood and he was instrumental in getting Wood to direct his next film, *For Whom the Bell Tolls* (1943), a film version of Hemingway's best seller that Paramount was considering—incredibly enough—as a Cecil B. DeMille spectacular.

After his starring role in *A Farewell to Arms,* Cooper had become a personal friend of Hemingway and he was the author's choice to play Robert Jordan, the American idealist who joins Loyalist guerrillas during the Spanish Civil War. The part of the girl, Maria, was not as easy to cast. Vera Zorina, the initial choice, was fired after two weeks of location work in Nevada and Ingrid Bergman became Maria, just like Hemingway had suggested from the start.

The chemistry was right between Bergman and Cooper: moviegoers shivered when she told him she wondered how noses fitted during a kiss. "Did you feel the earth move?" she asked him in a sly metaphor for

orgasm, and the public's well-adjusted seismograph registered the erotic tremor. Love scenes were never Cooper's strong suit, but with Bergman he ignited a cinematic bonfire that overshadowed the film's political angles, turning it into a romantic tour-de-force.

It was all for the best, since the screenplay had emasculated Hemingway's book. The rest of the cast never looked particularly Spanish and made up for it with some heavy overacting: Katina Paxinou, Akim Tamiroff, Mikhail Rasumny, Vladimir Sokoloff and Eric Feldary turned the film into a scene-stealing contest put on by a troupe of strolling players touring the Balkans and not the Sierra de Guadarrama.

Overlong and diluted as it was,

PRIDE OF THE YANKEES (1942). With Babe Ruth.

For Whom the Bell Tolls looked important and expensive enough to garner seven Academy Award nominations, including Cooper's fourth. Yet he had a lot of explaining to do to get back into Hemingway's graces: the novelist hated the film and for the next two decades one of the sure ways to test Hemingway's awesome gift for profanity was to mention director Sam Wood.

Wood may have irked Hemingway, but he had been splendid for Cooper and Bergman. Under his aegis they continued their screen partnership in *Saratoga Trunk*, a film version of Edna Ferber's trashy but readable best seller. Cast as Clio Dulaine, Bergman looked more seductive than ever in a black wig and there is electricity in the air as she flirtatiously sings in French to

101

Cooper, while caressing his cheek with a fan.

His part, much smaller than Bergman's, is as close as he would ever get to playing a Rhett Butler type. He manages fairly well as Clint Maroon, but is nowhere near Gable's leering rake mystique; the film is inarguably Bergman's. Amidst continuing rumors of a real-life romance between the stars, Warners was afraid that a double divorce scandal might hinder the wholesome pair, and temporarily shelved the picture. *Saratoga Trunk* was finished in 1943 and re-leased in 1945, when all danger was past.

Meanwhile, DeMille was busy casting Cooper in still another biography of a hero, *The Story of Dr. Wassell* (1944), inspired by the bravery of an Arkansas doctor who led a group of wounded Marines to safety during the war in the Pacific. DeMille glamorized the facts as much as he could, but he had to maintain a modicum of realism while dealing with contemporary history. The director's fanciful style was considerably cramped and the film, despite a visually stunning

FOR WHOM THE BELL TOLLS (1943). Robert Jordan with the guerrillas.

FOR WHOM THE BELL TOLLS (1943). Jordan takes aim at a soldier.

SARATOGA TRUNK (1945). With Ingrid Bergman.

THE STORY OF DR. WASSELL (1944). With Carol Thurston and wounded soldiers.

production, is one of the least beguiling DeMillean extravaganzas. Cooper is sensible, steady and not very interesting: the real Dr. Wassell was a much older man and not even DeMille could hoke up the material.

Cooper was then offered very advantageous financial terms to star in the first production of a new company, International Pictures, founded by scenarist Nunnally Johnson, producer William Goetz and ex-RKO president Leo Spitz.

He would work in a very congenial atmosphere with director Sam Wood and costar Teresa Wright, thus repeating the successful trio of *Pride of the Yankees.* But the end result of this friendly reunion was *Casanova Brown,* a very feeble comedy and one of Cooper's worst films.

Cooper plays a professor whose brief marriage to Teresa Wright has been annulled by her meddlesome, astrology-crazy mother (Patricia Collinge). On the eve of marrying

Anita Louise, he finds out there has been a "Little Accident," the original title of the twenties play on which Nunnally Johnson's screenplay was based. It had been filmed previously in 1930, with Douglas Fairbanks, Jr. and ZaSu Pitts, but the intervening years had eroded what small appeal its foolish plot may have contained.

The "Little Accident" means that Cooper had impregnated Wright during their brief hours together; she now pretends to put the child up for adoption, just to lure Cooper back. Cooper believes she really means it and, angry at her callousness, kidnaps the baby from the hospital. Hiding in a hotel suite, he turns into an idiotically overanxious father who frets because the infant has gained a pound in a week and at this rate will weigh a monstrous fifty-two pounds on her first birthday. Sam Wood directed all this with elephantine cuteness and Arthur Lange received an inexplicable Oscar nomination for the kind of unremittingly tinkly score that underlines nonexistent jokes, in a musical equivalent of television's canned laughter.

By 1945, after twelve years of marriage, Gary and Rocky Cooper

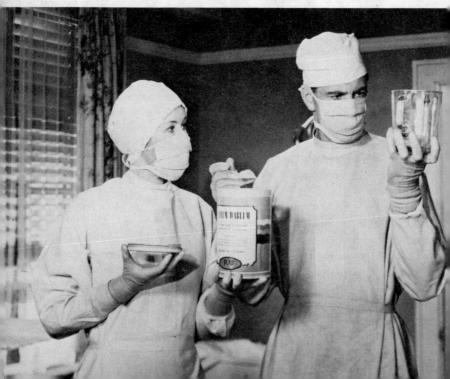

CASANOVA BROWN (1944). With Mary Treen.

ALONG CAME JONES (1945). With Loretta Young.

had slowly drifted apart. They travelled mostly in different circles and kept up with social appearances for the sake of their daughter Maria. It was a friendly, tolerant arrangement: Cooper was genuinely fond of Rocky and respected her sharp intelligence and business acumen. It was she who advised him to diversify his activities by becoming a producer in the easygoing, benevolent ambiance of International Pictures. The decision was a grave but unforeseeable mistake.

In *Along Came Jones* (1945), Cooper became his own producer, with Nunnally Johnson as scenarist and Stuart Heisler as director. Cooper lacked the ego and the stamina to function effectively in his new capacity. As he tried to please everyone on the set, the shooting schedule degenerated into chaos. Yet no one could have galvanized this snickering Western about a man who can't shoot but is mistaken for a gunfighter. In the end, the pitiful bumbler is saved when the girl (Loretta Young) has to take matters in hand and kill the villain.

Producer Cooper had wanted to cast another actor as Jones, and only stepped into the part at the last minute, to protect his investment. The film's basic situation demands an outright clown: Bob Hope, Joe E. Brown and Don Knotts have played similar roles in their careers. Straightforward Cooper was all wrong when facetiousness was mandatory. *Along Came Jones* was a flop and the last attempt at a disastrous merchandising scheme: Cooper selling Cooper.

After these misadventures with selecting the kind of fluff he personally favored, Cooper was more amenable to try a stronger theme.

He was intrigued with the part of the scientist in Fritz Lang's *Cloak and Dagger* (1946), one of Hollywood's first explorations of the post-atomic era. Lang modelled Cooper's role on Robert Oppenheimer, and the star cautioned writers Ring Lardner, Jr. and Albert Maltz that he "might get away with it, provided you keep the lines pretty short and don't give me too much intellectual stuff."

In *Cloak and Dagger*, Cooper is a physics professor recruited by the OSS to locate and free an atomic scientist held prisoner by the Nazis. Lang, one of the most irascible and exacting of directors, admired conscientious Cooper, who refused a double in fighting scenes that inten-

CLOAK AND DAGGER (1946). With Vladimir Sokoloff.

UNCONQUERED (1947). With Howard da Silva and Paulette Goddard.

sified his now chronic backaches. Lang concentrated his temper on costar Lilli Palmer and on producer Milton Sperling: the conspiracies in the plot pall by comparison with the intrigues that went on behind the camera.

Lang claims his whole purpose in making the film was its conclusion, in which Cooper found out that the Nazis had been on the point of creating their own atom bomb and somberly mused: "This is the year One of the atomic age and God help us if we think we can keep this secret from the world." The subject was very touchy and the whole last reel was discarded, leaving *Cloak and Dagger* as a kinetic but mindless spy melodrama.

In 1947, Cooper returned to Paramount for another Cecil B. DeMille pageant, *Unconquered*, with Paulette Goddard as the indentured slave he buys and with whom he survives countless perils, including a well-edited canoe ride down the rapids and an encounter with an amusingly improbable Boris Karloff in full Indian brave regalia. The film is sporadically exciting, but at two-and-a-half hours it demands the appetite for adventure, the suspension of disbelief and the strong sacroiliac of an audience of ten-year-olds.

Going down DeMille's rapids was nothing compared with the moral cliffhangers director Leo McCarey had in store for Cooper in *Good Sam*

(1948). Sinclair Lewis had refused to work on the screenplay, advising McCarey that any man who wanted to be an apostle in modern times was an idiot and the public would never sympathize with such a protagonist. Dauntless McCarey went on with *Good Sam*, short for Good Samaritan, a most peculiar comedy about a saintly fool whose guileless charity falls somewhere between Francis of Assisi and Buñuel's *Nazarin*.

Like *Nazarin*, Sam finds out that each and every one of his good deeds brings on catastrophe: he lends his car to a half-blind neighbor who smashes it and loses his job; he is almost run over while trying to stop a bus for a fat lady who had no

intention of boarding it; he crushes the last shreds of self-respect in the brother-in-law he supports so stiflingly that the sponger cries: "I'm here for contrast, to make other people look good."

Sam will not admit that as a one-man welfare state he is more hindrance than help. His generosity is a corrupting force and, worst of all, he ignores the principle that charity begins at home: he gives away his house-buying fund so that another couple can open a food stand. Ann Sheridan is excellent as the harassed wife who weeps at Sam's follies but is tart enough to recover with a quip. When the local parson tells her she'd make a striking fortune-teller at the church

GOOD SAM (1948). With Ann Sheridan.

bazaar, she cracks: "Yeah, gypsies have no homes." Sheridan's is the voice of sanity in a film where the Cooper image has levitated into altruistic dementia.

Good Sam is McCarey's foray into Capra territory, but this genial comedy director lacked Capra's hard-headed practicality: the same audience who adored *Mr. Deeds* turned their backs on Sam's loony-bin piety. At the end, Cooper is rescued from a drunken binge in a Salvation Army mission and made vice-president of the store that fired him, as all join in a boozy chorus of "Let Me Call You Sweetheart." The audience was far more cynical than McCarey and rejected this odd valentine to the perversity of total goodness.

Cooper was left on his own once more. His failure as an independent producer had made him distrust his freedom and long for authority. In this frame of mind he signed for a six picture deal with Warners. His wife Rocky, in a knotty twist of fate, advised him to ask the studio for the leading role in their upcoming version of Ayn Rand's deliriously individualistic novel, *The Fountainhead* (1948).

Warners had acquired the property as a Barbara Stanwyck vehicle, but director King Vidor thumbed down this choice. He considered Stanwyck neither young, sexy or attractive enough to play Dominique Francon and the part was given to an intense Broadway actress, Patricia Neal. Vidor also wanted a sarcastic and brusque actor like Bogart to play the rebellious architect, but he had to settle for Cooper. The star's presence had been so assiduously softened during the past decade that even sharp-eyed Vidor had forgotten the early Cooper performances, with their barely tapped veins of surliness and obstinacy.

These qualities, essential to the part of Howard Roark, quickly surfaced in Cooper and in this bizarre, paranoid movie he is able to maneuver through every turn of Ayn Rand's tortuous, vertiginous screenplay. King Vidor compressed huge chunks of crazy narrative into one of the fastest movies ever made, handling Miss Rand's laughable dialogue and situations with an audacity that amounts to artistic *chutzpah.*

The Fountainhead is visually stunning, with image after compelling image; skyscrapers float over Henry Hull's dying face through the window of an ambulance; empty desks in a deserted newspaper office are lit from above in a mortuary glare; Patricia Neal is all aflutter in sexy veils as she ogles Cooper from the top of a marble quarry. Then, in an unforgettable finale, she ascends in an open elevator to the summit of Cooper's most priapic structure, with the Empire State building dis-

THE FOUNTAINHEAD (1948). With Patricia Neal.

TASK FORCE (1949). As Captain Jonathan Scott.

solving below into a mere speck, as she rushes to a lovers' meeting somewhere in the lower stratosphere.

The Fountainhead is every bit as trashy as *Morocco*, and every bit as erotically powerful. Cooper and Neal writhe frantically in the throes of attraction-repulsion: she taunts him, he rapes her, she lashes him, he derides her, as Max Steiner's score weaves a symphonic mesh around them. The film is Vidor's Wagnerian freak, too foolish to admire comfortably, too brilliant to dismiss flippantly. It was a mere accident in Cooper's career but it was a turning point in his life.

Cooper fell in love with Patricia Neal and both were plunged, for more than two years, into a maelstrom of guilt, regret, fleeting happiness and underlying despair. A staunch Catholic, Rocky Cooper would not consider divorce, and there were endless recriminations, interminable interviews with lawyers and counselors. Cooper and Neal lived in seclusion, hounded by the press, while Hollywood society sided against him and many a door was closed in his face. The couple even travelled to Havana, desperately avoiding reporters, to seek approval from Ernest Hemingway, one of the few friends who showed sympathy for Cooper's predicament.

Cooper and Neal's careers disin-tegrated with their personal lives. Warners feared the public would not accept a spotless screen Cooper in the midst of this storm of adverse publicity. The studio resorted to starring him in action films of limited scope: *Task Force* (1949) was Delmer Daves' routine naval drama, only memorable for its fine World War II documentary footage in color, and Stuart Heisler's *Dallas* (1950) was a confused Western that started as a comedy and then erupted into fast action.

Even Raoul Walsh, potentially an ideal director for Cooper's larger-than-life heroic frame, failed to stimulate him in *Distant Drums* (1951), in which Cooper fights the Seminoles in the Everglades. This pseudo-historical action film looks suspiciously like a jungle movie: treacherous snakes and hungry alligators endanger Cooper's forces as they get lost in the swamp and the plot creeps to a climactic and Tarzan-like underwater knife duel between Cooper and the Indian chief. *Distant Drums* offers Cooper only one good scene, as he tells Mari Aldon of the death of his wife at the hands of drunken soldiers and of his stoical decision to live on without holding a grudge.

Warners was getting all the mileage possible out of Cooper's contract and guest-spotted him in Doris Day's *It's a Great Feeling* (1949) and in *Starlift* (1951), a clank-

DISTANT DRUMS (1951). Captain Wyatt grapples with an Indian.

ing musical about USO activities during the Korean War. One of the brightest moments of these grim years is his five minute monologue as a sly cowboy in *It's a Big Country* (1951). Written by Dorothy Kingsley and directed by Clarence Brown, the sketch has Cooper disclaiming all exaggerations about the size and power of Texas,. while film clips keep contradicting his words. There are elements of self-parody in his performance, as he consciously displays all his mannerisms and seems to be insinuating that—as with Texas—all you may have heard about Coop is not entirely true.

An exception to this series of man's pictures and innocuous bits is *Bright Leaf* (1950), his only other film with Patricia Neal. Perhaps inspired by Cooper's lean style, Miss Neal would later become one of the screen's finest actresses, but in *Bright Leaf* she was high-strung and theatrical as the cruel, half-mad wife Cooper deserts for a respectful prostitute (Lauren Bacall). Even an iron-fisted director like Michael Curtiz could not rein the wild melodramatics. The film tiptoed into general distribution as the Coopers announced a tentative separation.

Cooper looked tired and dispirited as he mechanically starred in the films of this barren period. He seems to be eschewing close-ups, averting his eyes, as if in fear that the camera would again turn enemy and photograph his confused thoughts. He was more guarded than ever in *U.S.S. Teakettle* (1951), a belated service comedy in which even Henry Hathaway could not bring him out of his protective shell.

In this film, an unsure, suspicious Cooper holds his cards too close to his chest as a "ninety day wonder" reservist called into active duty. He ineptly runs an experimental ship devised to work at top speed on a complicated steam engine. He only saves the day when he lifts the crew's morale in sequences that echo a then current Broadway hit, *Mr. Roberts.*

At the top of his form, Cooper would have been a fine *Mr. Roberts,* but in this poor imitation he never opened up, in a role that must buy audience sympathy with a forthright approach. The film was such a financial fiasco that it was shelved and re-released as *You're in the Navy Now.* It fared better under the new title but its one-joke plot was as sputtering and asthmatic as the steam engine it was built around.

By Christmas of 1951, Cooper and Neal gave up the struggle. The possibility of marriage was ever diminishing and neither could stand the strain of waiting for an unattainable ideal of respectability. Cooper's grief was a secret to no one and he poured the anguish of the

BRIGHT LEAF (1950). With Patricia Neal.

YOU'RE IN THE NAVY NOW (1951). With Jane Greer.

HIGH NOON (1952). As Marshal Will Kane.

past years into a cathartic film, *High Noon* (1952). All the geniality is gone from his cragged face, all the sweetness has vanished in his bitter, agonizing performance.

He plays Will Kane, Marshal of Hadleyville. On his last day on the job, Kane has married young Grace Kelly and is on his way to retirement. News filters into town; the desperadoes he has sent to jail have been released and are rushing back to kill him. He tries to leave with Kelly, but his steely sense of duty forces him to return, because he does not want "to lie like a coward in my grave." His furious bride is only the first one to turn on him.

Trying to organize a posse against the incoming brutes, Kane finds the town he valiantly defended is shunning him like a leper. Realizing that he must stand alone in an ultimate test of his manhood, he writes his last will and testament and then walks out to die as courageously as he lived. In the end, it is his young Quaker wife who violates her religious precepts by shooting one of the bandits. Kane rejects the repentant Hadleyville authorities who come to greet him and throws his Marshal's badge in the dust, at their feet.

The wounded ego, the innate sense of honor, the painful righteousness, the capacity for suffering that never crumbles into masochism: all the constants of the Gary Cooper character are heightened by Carl Foreman's spare screenplay and Fred Zinnemann's austere direction. Here is a man unprotestingly accepting betrayal, facing death and then surviving in a flash of self-preservation. *High Noon* compresses the Cooper Mythology into 96 minutes. He is Prometheus bound, devoured, unchained and bitter in his triumph. Sadder and wiser now, he played it with a new awareness in a flawless performance.

"It demanded everything I had," he said, "and I gave it all I had." As drained of emotion as Will Kane, Cooper turned his back on Hollywood after finishing the picture and drifted aimlessly through Europe, trying to recall his youthful days. Yet his belated rebellion left a taste of ashes in his mouth. He came back to his home town, to his job, to his movies. It was all he knew, all he had.

And when he was awarded his second Oscar for *High Noon*, he did not throw it scornfully in the dust like Will Kane's badge, but hugged it gratefully. His past and his present had become interchangeable. They would also become his future.

HIGH NOON (1952). With Grace Kelly.

Home was the hero—in professional triumph and personal defeat. *High Noon* had placed Cooper as the top box office attraction in the industry. The exiled monarch returned from Europe to reclaim his throne, but he could no longer fully enjoy his victory: doctors in Paris had diagnosed an ulcer, his first intimation of mortality, carved in his insides by the guilt, indecision and ultimate resignation of the past three years.

Cooper had missed his last chance at liberation and now had to face the final American blasphemy: he was getting old. His state of depression was deepened by routine films like Andre De Toth's *Springfield Rifle*, his last Western under his Warners contract. Cooper plays a Major in the Union's Army during the Civil War. He pretends to be a coward and is dishonorably discharged with a yellow streak painted down his back. He is being set up as a convincing spy to infiltrate the enemy camp, but only the high command knows the plan: his wife (Phyllis Thaxter) shuns him and his ashamed young son runs away from home. The Major's public and private life disintegrate and so does the film, switching between horse and soap opera.

There are so many double and triple crossings that *Springfield*

"HIGH NOON" TO SUNSET

Rifle is as difficult to describe and as tedious to watch as a marathon game of tic-tac-toe. There is a good climax as Cooper corners the real traitor (Paul Kelly) but after so many zigzagging betrayals, the audience no longer cares what side the characters are on. Cooper has to wait 89 minutes for his one reasonably effective line as he refuses to shoot Kelly and tells him: "I need you for living proof that five good men didn't die in vain."

In *Return to Paradise* (1953), Mark Robson's unconvincing version of James Michener's novel, Cooper is hammer-locked with a Puritan preacher (Barry Jones), in Polynesia. Cooper struggles to save the half-breed daughter he had spawned and left behind: as in the twenties, he was back to redeeming women, but now one generation removed. The age gap shackled him into performing his task not by physical love but by sermonizing.

Blowing Wild (1953), made right after American exhibitors had voted Cooper the year's box office champion, seems almost like a concerted effort to bring him down from this prominence. It is a turgid melo-

SPRINGFIELD RIFLE (1952). With Guinn Williams (at his right) and Martin Milner (with rifle).

RETURN TO PARADISE (1953). With Roberta Haynes.

BLOWING WILD (1953). With Anthony Quinn.

drama set to a caterwauling Frankie Laine title song and the ludicrously improbable screenplay has Barbara Stanwyck killing her husband (Anthony Quinn) in an attempt to renew an affair with Cooper, who is busy redeeming an erstwhile B-girl (Ruth Roman). The quadrangle was too old by several years for this sort of flaming passion and the stars were driven to hard-breathing excesses by Hugo Fregonese's fevered direction. Their notices sounded like get-well cards.

Henry Hathaway tried to reactivate a youthful rapport with his aging star in *Garden of Evil* (1954), but Cooper was only superficially engaged in this badly stitched sampler of cliches, in which Susan Hayward enlists him, Richard

Widmark and Cameron Mitchell in a search for her trapped husband (Hugh Marlowe), who had dared hunt for an accursed treasure in nineteenth-century Mexico.

Cooper is the dour hero, Widmark is the cynic turned sentimental and Mitchell plays the hothead. As in *The Lives of a Bengal Lancer* and *The Real Glory*, the brawling male trio is led into peril by a woman: it is the Hathaway mixture as before, but the ingredients had gone stale. When only Cooper and Hayward survive a final massacre preordained by Indian superstition, he is given a curtain speech against the lust for riches, ending with: "If the earth were made of gold, I guess men would die for a handful of dirt." This pseudo-philosophical tirade

GARDEN OF EVIL (1954). With Richard Widmark and Susan Hayward.

VERA CRUZ (1954). With Burt Lancaster.

was singled out by reviewers to score a film that worked well enough on a simple-minded action level, but had no right to turn preachy on such short notice.

Cooper stayed in Mexico for *Vera Cruz* (1954), in which he and Burt Lancaster play American mercenaries in the midst of the Mexican war of independence, shifting allegiances between *Juaristas* and Emperor Maximilian's troops. The blatantly inaccurate screenplay hovers between the hilarious and the infuriating, with its sombreroed peasants, Spanish flamenco dancers and arrogant dragoons, ready-mixed into a confused fandango. *Vera Cruz* was actually shot in the Mexican countryside but takes place deep in the chauvinistic heart of Hollywood.˙

The pace is lame and the script paraplegic, but director Robert Aldrich injects some vigor into the explosive battle scenes that kept the audience periodically awake. These wholesale massacres of falling horsemen would have made several extra dollars for stuntman Frank Cooper in the twenties, but they were small change for actor Gary Cooper. Within the circumstances, Aldrich gave Cooper as much deference as he could and the star's presence looms formidably as Ernest Laszlo's low-angled camera seems to be constantly on its knees before him.

But *Vera Cruz,* for what little it is worth, belongs to Burt Lancaster, who seduces Denise Darcel and performs many an acrobatic feat with a glittering, malevolent grin, as if his very teeth were high on adrenalin. It is a divertingly hammy performance that Aldrich tried vainly to control: co-producer Lancaster was on his way to directing himself as *The Kentuckian* and was trying his new britches on for size all over the location.

Despite Aldrich's obvious respect for Cooper's craft, he was only able to give him a fine silent moment when—after shooting Lancaster in the last gunfight—Cooper's grimace expresses self-hatred and regret at realizing his adversary's gun had not been loaded.

Gary Cooper was fifty-three. After his last stab at self-assertion and autumnal love with Patricia Neal, he had been left a very lonely man. His innate Puritan streak made him wince at publicity reports of his "romances" with French actress Giselle Pascal and model Lorraine Chanel. He was feeling ill and desperately wanted to rest quietly again. Maria, his fervently Catholic daughter, suggested an audience with the Pope: it was the first step to a reconciliation with his wife, and later Cooper, a life-long Episcopalian, received instruction in Catholicism and embraced Rocky and Maria's faith.

THE COURT-MARTIAL OF BILLY MITCHELL (1955). With James Daly and Ralph Bellamy.

As a man, Cooper had been brought back into the fold but this triggered a final, significant change in his attitude as an actor. His desire for a second chance in life slowly channelled itself into a search for newer, more challenging movie roles: in his last nine movies he tackled one atypical part after another, as if he no longer cared what people thought of Cooper, the star, as long as they acknowledged that Cooper, the actor, had expanded and grown.

In the last of his film biographies, Otto Preminger's *The Court-Martial of Billy Mitchell* (1956), he impersonates the annoying, visionary general who insisted on strengthening American air power and even predicted the Japanese attack on Pearl Harbor twenty years before the fact. This irascible "Cassandra in uniform"—as Mitchell was tagged—is a far cry from the forbearing, unilateral heroes of Cooper's heyday as a beloved star.

It is another ordeal of martyrdom

THE FRIENDLY PERSUASION (1956). With Anthony Perkins.

and sacrifice, as Mitchell deliberately insults his superiors to get himself court-martialed, just to promote his unpopular theories into a *cause célèbre* and focus public attention on his prophecies of doom. In this thorny role, Cooper is able to project a cantankerous man with gentle obstinacy that is devoid of arrogance, especially in the trial scenes when he faces a vicious antagonist (Rod Steiger) with none of the mute passivity of similar confrontations in *Mr. Deeds* and *Souls at Sea*. He adds a human dimension

to his perfervid Howard Roark of *The Fountainhead*, making Mitchell stubborn but likeable, obsessive yet rational.

Cooper is equally admirable in William Wyler's *The Friendly Persuasion* (1956). Before playing Wyler's *The Westerner* in 1940, he had been wary of being overshadowed in a lesser part, but this time he accepted a role that was no more than a brushstroke in Wyler's detailed fresco of Quaker life at the time of the Civil War. The film is a collection of vignettes where nothing and no one stands out: scenes are lined up like preserve jars in a pioneer's larder and there is no more emphasis on a restless child screaming "God is love" in an empty church than on Dorothy McGuire's perennial battle with Samantha, an obnoxious goose.

In a meandering, unpruned film Cooper patiently waits for almost two hours for the central conflict to emerge when his son (Anthony Perkins) defies the family's pacifist religion to take arms in the war. Then Cooper compassionately expresses the anxiety of a man at the crossroads between faith and family duty. *The Friendly Persuasion* won the Palme d'Or as best film at the Cannes Film Festival and ran neck-to-neck with *Around the World in Eighty Days* for the 1956 best film Oscar. There were a total of six Academy Award nominations for *The Friendly Persuasion*, including ones for Wyler and Perkins. Cooper was unjustly ignored.

In 1957, Billy Wilder cast Cooper in a role that was very similar to the one he had written for him in Lubitsch's disappointing *Bluebeard's Eighth Wife*. In Wilder's *Love in the Afternoon*, it is as if the flighty millionaire who had married Claudette Colbert in the early film had come back to Paris, a middle-aged roué, older and wiser by two decades.

It may be the same part, but it is a different Cooper who faces the challenge. He is no longer trying to fool anyone as a *faux naif* and he brings a surprisingly acid quality to the character. In *Love in the Afternoon* he is the plutocrat who collects glamorous fallen women with a rictus of disenchantment around his sated lips: he has sampled all the poisoned goodies and hopes against hope for the last breath of innocence he finds in spritely Audrey Hepburn.

Hepburn is Ariane, the daughter of Maurice Chevalier, a private detective with a juicily scandalous dossier on dangerous Cooper, who has recently been chosen Man of the Year by *Confidential* magazine. In her sheltered existence, angelic Ariane fashions the tycoon as the devil incarnate and develops a maidenly crush on him. When she finds out he is about to be shot by a jealous cuckold, she invades Cooper's suite at the Paris Ritz and pretends to be his five-to-seven date. The unfaithful wife makes a hasty retreat through the balcony and the gun-wielding husband (John McGiver) disappears in a flurry of apologies.

Pure, virginal Hepburn then poses as a *demi-mondaine*, telling Cooper about her numerous affairs with "export-import" moneybags who keep her in style. Ariane drives him nearly crazy with her sexy lies, while a schmaltzy violin quartet, hired for each of Cooper's seductions, constantly plays "Fascination" as a maddening *leitmotif* for his fury at not being able to snare this elusive prey.

Love in the Afternoon is another of Wilder's wicked inversions of bedtime stories and in the last funny-touching scene, Red Riding Hood devours the Wolf. The film is so seemingly cold, so deceptively wry that it never cloys: it is molasses and vinegar all the way. Wilder appropriately dedicated it to Lubitsch, for it is one of the high points of the kind of romantic comedy that was Vienna's gift to Hollywood. With a charm that never wilts, the film has an ever-strengthening claim to be called a masterpiece.

Throughout *Love in the Afternoon*, Wilder had been exquisitely careful to hide the unmistakable erosions of time in Cooper's face. Gauzy filters were used, and crucial love scenes were shot with the camera poised behind Cooper's shoulder. Reviewers, while admiring Cooper's skill, prudently suggested that he was too old for his role. Then, in 1958, he underwent what

LOVE IN THE AFTERNOON (1957). With Audrey Hepburn.

was described as "minor facial surgery." No strong denials could scotch the rumors that he had had his face lifted and that the operation had not been successful. Whether true or false, all this talk is important in providing a clue to the inner mechanism of his next performance in *Ten North Frederick* (1958).

The film is not remotely as good as *Love in the Afternoon*, but Cooper is even better in this, the first role where his advancing age is not only admitted and discussed but plays an integral part in the drama. John O'Hara's novel had been acquired by Fox for Spencer Tracy.

When he shied away from it, Cooper agreed to play Joe Chapin, an honest man with presidential aspirations, brought down by a shrewish wife (Geraldine Fitzgerald), an irresponsible daughter (Diane Varsi) and a poignant love affair with the daughter's college roommate (Suzy Parker).

O'Hara's fine novel chronicled the downfall of a Wendell Willkie type of populist candidate, crushed by chicanery and high power politics. Philip Dunne's screenplay eliminated most of O'Hara's detailed background and Cooper's May-December romance with Suzy

LOVE IN THE AFTERNOON (1957). With Audrey Hepburn.

TEN NORTH FREDERICK (1958) With Suzy Parker.

Parker became the film's inner core and saving grace. Joe Chapin is not a lecher but a middle-aged romantic trying to recapture his faded youth in a pathetic last fling with a sensitive girl. On screen, Cooper seems to be living the dilemma of his difficult years and he brings a heart-rending dignity to Chapin, a character described as "a gentleman in a time that has no place for gentlemen."

Philip Dunne's direction of his own screenplay is very uneven. The film is sometimes stodgy and visually uninteresting, but Dunne can be credited with inspiring Cooper and animating the wooden Miss Parker in her only good performance. In their finest scene, they part over a semantic misunderstanding. She apologizes because she did not mean to have pried into his personal life, but he reacts by telling her it is a matter of pride for him: he must stop dallying with a girl young enough to be his daughter. There is a real emotional charge

TEN NORTH FREDERICK (1958). With Geraldine Fitzgerald.

as she spells the word, assuring him she meant "p-r-i-e-d" and he holds on to his wrenching "p-r-i-d-e." Chapin gives up his one true love and dies, after a life of quiet desperation. Then daughter Varsi—in a very moving ending—thanks Suzy Parker for having given her father his only happy day.

Cooper's haggard face in *Ten North Frederick* shocked audiences. His strength was failing and doctors advised him to slow down, but he kept going full tilt against those windmills. There was another exciting challenge in Anthony Mann's *Man of the West* (1958). Reginald Rose's screenplay offered Cooper the chance to play an ambiguous character, almost an anti-hero: Link Jones is the reformed bandit who pretends to rejoin the gang run by his sadist uncle Tobin (Lee J. Cobb).

Jones is only trying to gain time to save the captive stagecoach passenger (Julie London), but when they all ride into a ghost town his character becomes increasingly complex. He is gradually infected by the madness in Cobb and his evil henchman (Jack Lord). By close contact with his brutal past, Link Jones feels all the layers of sanity, morality and civilization are being stripped from him. He is both excited and ashamed when the caveman instinct surfaces in him and he admits to Julie London: "I want to kill all the Tobins and that makes me just like they are."

Psychological Westerns were enjoying a vogue in the fifties and Cooper was venturing into new areas. He had the right guide in Anthony Mann. The director liked to work with screen idols and had a curious theory about them. "It's all in the eyes," he told *Cahiers du Cinema* when he dissected Cooper's performance in *Man of the West*. "The heroes, all the stars that the public loves, have very light blue or green eyes. Think of Clark Gable, James Stewart, Robert Taylor, John Wayne, Burt Lancaster, Henry Fonda, Paul Newman, Charlton Heston, Peter O'Toole . . . the eyes reflect the inner flame that animates the heroes. The guys with dark eyes play supporting roles or become character actors."

In *Man of the West*, Mann used Cooper to expound this quasi-metaphysical approach to male stardom, yet this Freudian Western fell victim to insensitive reviews and grind distribution. Cooper's next film, however, far exceeded box office expectations and turned into a "sleeper" for Warners. *The Hanging Tree* (1959) finally realizes Cooper's potential for mystery and menace, the qualities he was often denied in his youth and which were surfacing in his very last films. Cooper is at his laconic best as a doc-

MAN OF THE WEST (1958). With Julie London.

tor with an ominous past, thrown into a Montana silver lode vendetta that involves a temporarily blind girl (Maria Schell), an impressionable young fellow (Ben Piazza) and a neurotic villain (Karl Malden).

Cooper's hip was now intensely painful and kept him from compli-

cated riding scenes. The award-winning novella by Dorothy M. Johnson could not be disfigured by strong doses of excessive action. Scenarists Wendell Mayes and Halsted Welles did a commendable job of expanding the slender book by concentrating on the characters' psychological motivations, and director Delmer Daves went back to the brooding style of *Dark Passage* and *The Red House*, his early promising thrillers. *The Hanging Tree* is a very eclectic film that goes from an almost impressionistic stagecoach raid to semi-documentary sequences about life around the silver mine called "The Lucky Lady." All the disparate elements are held together by Cooper's reactions to Schell, Piazza and Malden: he gave the film a solid center that accounts for its unexpected box office strength.

All during the shooting of *The Hanging Tree*, Cooper was tired and visibly ill. There was fear that he would not be able to finish the picture. The anxiety took its toll on director Daves, who had to be hos-

THE HANGING TREE (1959). With Maria Schell.

THEY CAME TO CORDURA (1959). With Richard Conte, Van Heflin, and Dick York.

pitalized with an ulcer. Karl Malden had to double as director during the last week, following Daves' instructions and sketches. After *The Hanging Tree*, Cooper promised doctors to rest for a while, but then he read the screenplay by Robert Rossen and Ivan Moffat from Glendon Swarthout's novel *They Came to Cordura*. It was a challenge he could not shy away from.

The protagonist, Major Thomas Thorn, is a man in a lunatic quest for the secret of abstract courage. Like an alchemist of the mind, Thorn is trying to isolate the elusive element that makes some men shine in combat while others go into cowardly eclipse. Gary Cooper could not fail to respond to a film that promised to be the definitive analysis of the heroic mystique he had embodied for over three decades on the screen.

They Came to Cordura (1959) takes place in 1916, during America's punitive action against Pancho Villa. The country is on the brink of World War I and needs live heroes to set an example. The screenplay sends Cooper back to *Sergeant York* territory, but this

THEY CAME TO CORDURA (1959). With Rita Hayworth.

time he is not going to be the hero but the obsessed bystander. Colonel Rogers (Robert Keith) appoints Major Thorn as awards officer and orders him to select the men to receive the Congressional Medal of Honor. The job is a form of blackmail. Thorn's one moment of hesitation in battle has been sternly interpreted as cowardice. The Colonel suggests it will not go into Thorn's record if Thorn recommends him for the decoration that will secure his promotion to general.

Cooper defies Keith and picks five other men instead. They have distinguished themselves in a suicide attack on a Mexican garrison. Cooper questions them one by one, trying to find the quality they possess and he lacked. Singlemindedly he pursues the ungraspable as he half orders, half begs Lieutenant Fowler (Tab Hunter) to give him a clue: "I have a chance to put my hand on the bare heart of heroism," Major Thorn insists.

The Colonel senses Thorn is about to spring the lid of Pandora's box. With his five "heroes" he is sent on a hazardous trek to the town of Cordura: it is clear the Colonel does not expect them to reach their destination alive. Cooper is left alone with the men who fill him with awe and envy. As played by Van Heflin, Richard Conte, Michael Callan, Tab Hunter and Dick York, they soon reveal themselves as weaklings and varmints.

Rita Hayworth, a woman accused of consorting with the enemy, is to be their ward during the journey. She infuriates the men by flaunting the cigarettes and tequila she acquired from the Mexicans. Van Heflin, as the worst of the lot, wants to rape and demean her. Cooper must then fight sleep and exhaustion to defend the woman he secretly despises for being as intrinsically weak as he figures himself to be.

As it progresses to a hallucinatory climax, *They Came to Cordura* is not really a conflict between bravery and cowardice, but between good and evil on a stark raving mad level. This derailed film of great promise was disowned by director Rossen, who claimed it had been edited by the studio into a meaningless farrago. Rossen died in the midst of the fight to get the studio to restore the picture to his original

THE WRECK OF THE MARY DEARE (1959). With Charlton Heston.

conception. He left behind him a maddening film, so near and yet so far from its inherent brilliance.

It is also a ghostly, haunting film: Cooper was physically depleted while making it, and Major Thorn's struggle through the desert becomes a metaphor for Cooper's determination to finish it at all costs. When one sees him pull a wagon by a rope on slippery railroad tracks, reality overtakes fiction in a sequence that is almost unbearable to watch. Thorn has become Cooper. Both are pushing themselves beyond endurance in an insane compulsion to reach *Cordura:* it is significant that the name of the town is also the Spanish word for sanity.

Truth had to be faced at last and when *Cordura* was reached and the film completed, Gary Cooper entered a Hollywood hospital for abdominal surgery. Six weeks later, barely recovered, he was flown to a Boston clinic for a prostate operation. Cancer was now spreading through his system. Another man would have passively waited for the inevitable. Not Gary Cooper. He went on, waging the losing battle to the very end.

He was back before the cameras in *The Wreck of the Mary Deare* (1959) as Gideon Patch, a man accused of deliberately trying to sink a burning ship during a storm in the English Channel. The film is a harsher, more despairing version of *Souls at Sea,* as Patch incriminates himself by keeping silent about his real motives during the investigation. Then, in an underwater finale, Cooper and costar Charlton Heston finally solve the riddle of the Mary Deare.

Eric Ambler wrote a taut screenplay, based on a Hammond Innes novel. Cooper and Heston play well together and director Michael Anderson keeps the film afloat on a steady, adventurous course. But it was Cooper's last try at the genre: strong action pictures were no longer possible for him and Robert Mitchum replaced him in Zinnemann's *The Sundowners* when it became clear Cooper's ill health could not withstand the rigors of location in Australia. He was deeply hurt to miss the chance of doing this fine film, the one that should have capped his movie career. He had to face the last indignity for a film star: he was uninsurable.

He went to London instead for a sedate picture. It was *The Naked Edge,* made in late 1960 and released after his death in 1961. In his last film, Gary Cooper was still trying to stretch his screen image to the utmost. He told interviewers that he welcomed the project—the one murder mystery in his long career—because he was curious to see whether audiences would accept him as a potential assassin.

THE NAKED EDGE (1961). With Deborah Kerr and Eric Portman.

He was never to find out how badly the experiment failed.

As George Radcliffe, an American sales representative in England, he gives very evasive testimony at a robbery and murder trial involving a business associate. His wife (Deborah Kerr) suspects that Cooper may be the culprit. A blackmail note confirms her doubts and she lives in fear that she might be the next victim. When *The Naked Edge* opened in New York,

the studio tried to increase the film's box office lure by barring audiences from entering the theatre during the last thirteen minutes: movie-goers were expected to believe that Cooper was waiting behind a door, ready to slit Kerr's throat. Of course, it was villain Eric Portman who lurked, razor in hand, foiled at the last minute by Cooper's intervention.

Cooper had been right in his misgivings. No suspense could be built around the impossibility of his playing a killer. His brooding performance is stealthy and menacing enough: if he were a newcomer the film would have worked. But even posthumously his screen image undermined his proficiency as an actor. *The Naked Edge* is very reminiscent of *Suspicion,* where Alfred Hitchcock had a similar problem with Cary Grant as a would-be assassin neither the studio nor the audience would tolerate. Michael Anderson, again directing Cooper, lacked Hitchcock's style and could not save a film that pivoted around an untenable premise.

Deborah Kerr remembers Cooper on the set of *The Naked Edge* as "a darling man, extremely thoughtful to work with, but he must have already been a very sick man. Sometimes he seemed withdrawn and remote, as though he were no longer with us." Shortly after finishing the picture, in December, 1960, Cooper was told that he had inoperable lung cancer. He stoically started to prepare himself for death.

On January 8, 1961, he was honored by his colleagues at a dinner in the Friar's Club in Hollywood. Audrey Hepburn recited a poem she wrote for him, specially for the occasion. Carl Sandburg called him "the world's most beloved illiterate." They were all around him: the stars, the directors, the producers.

They knew that Cooper was going and that with him a part of the Hollywood legend would be irretrievably gone. Then, to a stunned audience of his peers, Cooper said, smiling from the podium just as bravely as in *Pride of the Yankees:* "Today I consider myself the luckiest man on the face of this earth."

Compulsively, he went on being Coop until there was no more to give. On February, 1961, he flew to New York to narrate *The Real West*, a television documentary. He could work only a couple of hours at a time, returning to his hotel room to lie under an oxygen tent and then come back to the recording studio to read another page of the script. Many doubted he would finish it, but he did. Even as late as April 9, five weeks before his death, he was scheduled to appear on Dinah Shore's television show. This was the one professional date he had to cancel: he just could not go through with it.

Hollywood knew Cooper was dying but the rest of the world was shocked into realizing the truth on the night of April 20, during the Academy Awards presentation. Cooper had been voted a third, honorary Oscar and James Stewart walked on stage to accept it for him. Suddenly, Stewart's voice broke and before millions of televiewers he sobbed: "We're all very proud of

140

you, Coop, all of us are terribly proud." On May 14, 1961, seven days after his sixtieth birthday, it was all over.

"They can kill me off," Bogart had once wryly said, "but Cooper can't be killed off at the end." It was true: audiences would not have it, throughout Cooper's thirty-five years of stardom, so full of false reports of his death, improbable rescues, reassuring resurrections. This time, the unthinkable had happened. Newspapers carried the headline: GARY COOPER IS DEAD.

Or is he?

Last week I met a frightened, harassed friend who was on his way to a crucial confrontation. Not a movie character, but a real man in a bind, facing unjust enemies bent on bringing him down. He had very little going for him, except that he was right. As he sipped his last hurried cup of coffee, he smiled nervously and whispered: "God, I feel like Gary Cooper in *High Noon*." It worked like magic. His shoulders straightened, he raised his chin, adjusted his tie, clutched his briefcase close to his hip, put on a brave grin and strode on, down the canyons of Wall Street. It was Hadleyville once again.

Cooper is gone, but the ideal lives on: he can still be our amulet against despair, fear or adversity. No one dare blame him for the dreams he sold: like Willy Loman's, they came with his territory. Cooper died for our sins—but not in vain.

THE FILMS OF GARY COOPER

The director's name follows the release date. A (c) following the release date indicates that the film was in color. Sp indicates Screenplay and b/o indicates based/on.

Gary Cooper's early period as stuntman, extra and bit player includes appearances in nearly fifty films. Of these, the most important are: *The Thundering Herd, Wild Horse Mesa, Tricks, The Lucky Horseshoe, The Vanishing American, Three Pals* and *The Eagle,* all released in 1925, and *Lightnin' Wins, Watch Your Wife* and *The Enchanted Hill,* released in 1926. His starring career begins properly with *The Winning of Barbara Worth* (1926).

1. THE WINNING OF BARBARA WORTH, A Goldwyn Production, released by United Artists, 1926, *Henry King.* Sp: Frances Marion, b/o novel by Harold Bell Wright. Cast: Ronald Colman, Vilma Banky.

2. ARIZONA BOUND, Paramount, 1927, *John Waters.* Sp: John Stone, Paul Gangelin, b/o story by Richard Allen Gates, adapted by Marion Jackson. Cast: Betty Jewell, Paul Dougherty, El Brendel, Guinn "Big Boy" Williams.

3. NEVADA, Paramount, 1927, *John Waters.* Sp: John Stone, L.G. Rigby, b/o novel by Zane Grey. Cast: Thelma Todd, William Powell.

4. THE LAST OUTLAW, Paramount, 1927, *Arthur Rosson.* Sp: John Stone, J. Walter Ruben, b/o story by Richard Allen Gates. Cast: Betty Jewell, Jack Luden.

5. IT, Paramount, 1927, *Clarence Badger.* Sp: Hope Loring, Louis D. Lighton, from Elinor Glyn's adaptation of her novel. Cast: Clara Bow, Antonio Moreno.

6. CHILDREN OF DIVORCE, Paramount, 1927, *Frank Lloyd.* Sp: Hope Loring, Louis D. Lighton, b/o novel by Owen Johnson. Cast: Clara Bow, Esther Ralston, Einar Hanson, Hedda Hopper.

7. WINGS, Paramount, 1927, *William A. Wellman.* Sp: Hope Loring, Louis D. Lighton, b/o story by John Monk Saunders. Cast: Clara Bow, Charles "Buddy" Rogers, Richard Arlen, Jobyna Ralston, El Brendel, Henry B. Walthall, Hedda Hopper.

8. BEAU SABREUR, Paramount, 1928, *John Waters*. Sp: Tom J. Geraghty, b/o novel by Percival Christopher Wren. Cast: Evelyn Brent, Noah Beery, William Powell.

9. THE LEGION OF THE CONDEMNED, Paramount, 1928, *William A. Wellman*. Sp: John Monk Saunders, Jean de Limur, b/o story by John Monk Saunders. Cast: Fay Wray, Barry Norton.

10. DOOMSDAY, Paramount, 1928, *Rowland V. Lee*. Sp: Donald W. Lee, b/o novel by Warwick Deeping. Cast: Florence Vidor, Lawrence Grant.

11. HALF A BRIDE, Paramount, 1928, *Gregory La Cava*. Sp: Doris Anderson, Percy Heath, b/o story "White Hands" by Arthur Stringer. Cast: Esther Ralston, William J. Worthington, Freeman Wood.

12. LILAC TIME, First National, 1928, *George Fitzmaurice*. Sp: Carey Wilson, b/o play by Jane Cowl and Jane Murfin and book by Guy Fowler. Cast: Colleen Moore, Eugenie Besserer, Burr McIntosh.

13. THE FIRST KISS, Paramount, 1928, *Rowland V. Lee*. Sp: John Farrow, b/o story "Four Brothers" by Tristram Tupper. Cast: Fay Wray, Lane Chandler, Leslie Fenton.

14. THE SHOPWORN ANGEL, Paramount, 1928, *Richard Wallace*. Sp: Howard Estabrook, Albert Shelby LeVino, b/o story "Private Pettigrew's Girl" by Dana Burnet. Cast: Nancy Carroll, Paul Lukas. Remade in 1938 with James Stewart, Margaret Sullavan, Walter Pidgeon.

15. WOLF SONG, Paramount, 1929, *Victor Fleming*. Sp: John Farrow, Keene Thompson, b/o story by Harvey Fergusson. Cast: Lupe Velez, Louis Wolheim, Russ Columbo.

16. BETRAYAL, Paramount, 1929, *Lewis Milestone*. Sp: Hans Kraly, Leo Birinsky, b/o story by Victor Schertzinger and Nicholas Soussanin. Cast: Emil Jannings, Esther Ralston.

17. THE VIRGINIAN, Paramount, 1929, *Victor Fleming*. Sp: Howard Estabrook, b/o novel by Owen Wister and play by Owen Wister and Kirk LaShelle. Cast: Walter Huston, Richard Arlen, Mary Brian, Chester Conklin, Eugene Pallette. Previously filmed as a silent in 1914 with Dustin Farnum and in 1923 with Kenneth Harlan. Remade with Joel McCrea in 1946 and with James Drury as a television series in 1962.

18. ONLY THE BRAVE, Paramount, 1930, *Frank Tuttle*. Sp: Edward E. Paramore, Jr., b/o story by Keene Thompson. Cast: Mary Brian, Phillips Holmes.

19. THE TEXAN, Paramount, 1930, *John Cromwell*. Sp: Daniel N. Rubin, b/o Oliver Garrett's adaptation of "A Double-Dyed Deceiver" by O. Henry. Cast: Fay Wray, Emma Dunn. Remade in 1939 as *The Llano Kid* with Tito Guizar.

20. SEVEN DAYS LEAVE, Paramount, 1930, *Richard Wallace*. Sp: John Farrow, Dan Totheroh, b/o the play *The Old Lady Shows Her Medals* by J.M. Barrie. Cast: Beryl Mercer, Daisy Belmore.

21. A MAN FROM WYOMING, Paramount, 1930, *Rowland V. Lee*. Sp: John V. X.A.Weaver, Albert Shelby LeVino, b/o story by Joseph Moncure March and Lew Lipton. Cast: June Collyer, Regis Toomey, Morgan Farley.

22. THE SPOILERS, Paramount, 1930, *Edwin Carewe*. Sp: Agnes Brand Leahy, Bartlett Cormack, b/o novel by Rex Beach. Cast: Kay Johnson, Betty Compson, William Boyd, Slim Summerville. Filmed as a silent in 1914 with William Farnum; in 1923 with Milton Sills, Noah Beery and Anna Q. Nilsson. Remade in 1942 with Marlene Dietrich, John Wayne, Randolph Scott; in 1955 with Rory Calhoun, Anne Baxter and Jeff Chandler.

23. MOROCCO, Paramount, 1930, *Josef von Sternberg*. Sp: Jules Furthman, b/o novel *Amy Jolly* by Benno Vigny. Cast: Marlene Dietrich, Adolphe Menjou, Francis MacDonald, Eve Southern.

24. FIGHTING CARAVANS, Paramount, 1931, *Otto Brower, David Burton*. Sp: Edward E. Paramore, Jr., Keene Thompson, Agnes Brand Leahy, b/o novel by Zane Grey. Cast: Lily Damita, Tully Marshall, Eugene Pallette, James Farley, Jane Darwell.

25. CITY STREETS, Paramount, 1931, *Rouben Mamoulian*. Sp: Oliver H.P. Garrett and Max Marcin, b/o original screen treatment by Dashiell Hammett. Cast: Sylvia Sidney, William Boyd, Guy Kibbee, Paul Lukas.

26. I TAKE THIS WOMAN, Paramount, 1931, *Marion Gering, Slavko Vorkapich*. Sp: Vincent Lawrence, b/o novel by Mary Roberts Rinehart. Cast: Carole Lombard, Charles Trowbridge, Helen Ware, Lester Vail, Clara Blandick.

27. HIS WOMAN, Paramount, 1931, *Edward Sloman*. Sp: Adelaide Heilbron, Melville Baker, b/o novel by Dale Collins. Cast: Claudette Colbert, Douglas Dumbrille.

28. DEVIL AND THE DEEP, Paramount, 1932, *Marion Gering*. Sp: Benn Levy, b/o story by Harry Hervey. Cast: Tallulah Bankhead, Charles Laughton, Cary Grant, Paul Porcasi, Juliette Compton.

29. IF I HAD A MILLION, Paramount, 1932. *Norman McLeod* directed the Cooper sketch in an all-star film with cast including Charles Laughton, George Raft, May Robson, Mary Boland, Wynne Gibson, Frances Dee, Charles Ruggles, Alison Skipworth, Gene Raymond, *et. al.* Joyce Compton, Jack Oakie and Roscoe Karns appear in the Cooper sketch.

30. A FAREWELL TO ARMS, Paramount, 1932, *Frank Borzage.* Sp: Oliver H.P. Garrett, Benjamin Glazer, b/o novel by Ernest Hemingway. Cast: Helen Hayes, Adolphe Menjou, Mary Phillips, Jack LaRue. Remade in 1958 with Jennifer Jones and Rock Hudson.

31. TODAY WE LIVE, MGM, 1933, *Howard Hawks.* Sp: Edith Fitzgerald, Dwight Taylor, from William Faulkner's adaptation of his story "Turnabout." Cast: Joan Crawford, Robert Young, Franchot Tone, Roscoe Karns, Louise Closser Hale.

32. ONE SUNDAY AFTERNOON, Paramount, 1933, *Stephen Roberts.* Sp: William Slavens McNutt, Grover Jones, b/o play by James Hagan. Cast: Fay Wray, Frances Fuller, Neil Hamilton, Roscoe Karns, Jane Darwell. Remade in 1941 as *Strawberry Blonde* with James Cagney, Rita Hayworth, Olivia de Havilland, and in 1948 under original title in musical version with Dennis Morgan, Dorothy Malone and Janis Paige.

33. DESIGN FOR LIVING, Paramount, 1933, *Ernst Lubitsch.* Sp: Ben Hecht, b/o play by Noel Coward. Cast: Fredric March, Miriam Hopkins, Edward Everett Horton.

34. ALICE IN WONDERLAND, Paramount, 1933, *Norman McLeod.* Sp: Joseph L. Mankiewicz, William Cameron Menzies, b/o the Lewis Carroll "Alice" novels. Cast: W.C. Fields, Edna May Oliver, Charlotte Henry, Charles Ruggles, Ned Sparks, Cary Grant, Leon Errol, Edward Everett Horton, Richard Arlen, May Robson, Ethel Griffies, Jack Oakie, Raymond Hatton, Louise Fazenda, Sterling Holloway.

35. OPERATOR 13, MGM; 1933, *Richard Boleslavsky.* Sp: Harry Thew, Zelda Sears, Eve Greene, b/o story by Robert W. Chambers. Cast: Marion Davies, Jean Parker, Katharine Alexander, Douglas Dumbrille.

36. NOW AND FOREVER, Paramount, 1934, *Henry Hathaway.* Sp: Vincent Lawrence, Sylvia Thalberg, b/o story by Jack Kirkland and Melville Baker. Cast: Shirley Temple, Carole Lombard, Sir Guy Standing, Charlotte Granville, Gilbert Emery.

37. THE WEDDING NIGHT, A Goldwyn Production, released by United Artists, 1935. *King Vidor.* Sp: Edith Fitzgerald, b/o story by Edwin Knopf. Cast: Anna Sten, Helen Vinson, Ralph Bellamy, Siegfried Rumann.

38. THE LIVES OF A BENGAL LANCER, Paramount, 1935, *Henry Hathaway*.
Sp: John L. Balderston, Waldemar Young, Achmed Abdullah, b/o novel by
Major Francis Yeats-Brown. Cast: Franchot Tone, Richard Cromwell, Sir Guy
Standing, Douglas Dumbrille, C. Aubrey Smith, Kathleen Burke.

39. PETER IBBETSON, Paramount, 1935, *Henry Hathaway*. Sp: Vincent Law-
rence, Waldemar Young, b/o novel by George DuMaurier and play by John
Nathaniel Raphael. Cast: Ann Harding, John Halliday, Ida Lupino, Virginia
Weidler, Douglas Dumbrille, Doris Lloyd, Donald Meek. Remake of a George
Fitzmaurice 1922 version under the title *Forever*, with Wallace Reid and Elsie
Ferguson.

40. DESIRE, Paramount, 1936, *Frank Borzage*. Sp: Waldemar Young, Edwin
Justus Mayer, Samuel Hoffenstein, b/o play by Hans Szekely and R.A.
Stemmle. Cast: Marlene Dietrich, John Halliday, William Frawley, Akim
Tamiroff, Alan Mowbray. Remake of 1933 German film *Beautiful Days in
Aranjuez*, with Brigitte Helm.

41. MR. DEEDS GOES TO TOWN, Columbia, 1936, *Frank Capra*. Sp: Robert
Riskin, b/o story by Clarence Budington Kelland. Cast: Jean Arthur, Lionel
Stander, George Bancroft, Douglas Dumbrille, Raymond Walburn, Walter
Catlett.

42. THE GENERAL DIED AT DAWN, Paramount, 1936, *Lewis Milestone*. Sp:
Clifford Odets, b/o novel by Charles G. Booth. Cast: Madeleine Carroll, Akim
Tamiroff, Porter Hall, William Frawley.

43. THE PLAINSMAN, Paramount, 1936, *Cecil B. DeMille*. Sp: Waldemar Young,
Harold Lamb, Lynn Riggs, b/o stories by Frank J. Wilstach and *Prince of
Pistoleers* by Courtney Ryley Cooper and Grover Jones. Cast: Jean Arthur,
James Ellison, Helen Burgess, Porter Hall, Anthony Quinn. Remade in 1966
with Don Murray.

44. SOULS AT SEA, Paramount, 1937, *Henry Hathaway*. Sp: Dale Van Every,
Grover Jones, b/o story by Ted Lesser. Cast: George Raft, Frances Dee, Henry
Wilcoxon, Olympe Bradna, Porter Hall, Robert Cummings, Virginia Weidler,
Joseph Schildkraut, Harry Carey, George Zucco.

45. THE ADVENTURES OF MARCO POLO, A Goldwyn Production, released
by United Artists, 1938, *Archie Mayo*. Sp: Robert E. Sherwood, b/o story by
N.A. Pogson. Cast: Sigrid Gurie, Ernest Truex, Binnie Barnes, Alan Hale,
Basil Rathbone, George Barbier, Lana Turner.

46. BLUEBEARD'S EIGHTH WIFE, Paramount, 1938, *Ernst Lubitsch*. Sp:
Charles Brackett, Billy Wilder, b/o play by Alfred Savoir. Cast: Claudette
Colbert, Edward Everett Horton, David Niven, Franklin Pangborn, Herman
Bing, Elizabeth Patterson.

47. THE COWBOY AND THE LADY, A Goldwyn Production, released by United Artists, 1938, *H.C. Potter*. Sp: S.N. Behrman, Sonya Levien, b/o story by Leo McCarey and Frank R. Adams. Cast: Merle Oberon, Walter Brennan, Patsy Kelly, Harry Davenport, Mabel Todd, Fuzzy Knight, Emma Dunn.

48. BEAU GESTE, Paramount, 1939, *William A. Wellman*. Sp: Robert Carson, b/o novel by Percival C. Wren. Cast: Robert Preston, Ray Milland, Susan Hayward, Brian Donlevy, J. Carrol Naish, Albert Dekker, James Stephenson, Broderick Crawford. Filmed in silent version in 1926 with Ronald Colman and remade in 1966 with Guy Stockwell.

49. THE REAL GLORY, A Goldwyn Production, released by United Artists, 1939, *Henry Hathaway*. Sp: Jo Swerling, Robert R. Presnell, b/o story by Charles L. Clifford. Cast: David Niven, Andrea Leeds, Broderick Crawford, Reginald Owen, Kay Johnson, Tetsu Komai, Elvira Rios.

50. THE WESTERNER, A Goldwyn Production, released by United Artists, 1940, *William Wyler*. Sp: Jo Swerling, Niven Busch, b/o story by Stuart N. Lake. Cast: Doris Davenport, Walter Brennan, Forrest Tucker, Chill Wills, Lillian Bond, Lupita Tovar.

51. NORTH WEST MOUNTED POLICE, Paramount, 1940, (c), *Cecil B. DeMille*. Sp: Alan LeMay, Jesse Lasky, Jr., C. Gardner Sullivan, b/o "Royal Canadian Mounted Police" by R.C. Fetherston Haugh. Cast: Madeleine Carroll, Robert Preston, Paulette Goddard, Preston Foster, George Bancroft, Lynne Overman, Akim Tamiroff, Lon Chaney, Jr., Walter Hampden.

52. MEET JOHN DOE, Warners, 1941, *Frank Capra*. Sp: Robert Riskin, b/o story by Robert Presnell and Richard Connell. Cast: Barbara Stanwyck, Edward Arnold, Walter Brennan, James Gleason, Spring Byington, Gene Lockhart, Regis Toomey, Rod La Rocque, Ann Doran, Sterling Holloway.

53. SERGEANT YORK, Warners, 1941, *Howard Hawks*. Sp: John Huston, Harry Chandlee, Howard Koch, Abem Finkel, b/o the diary of Sgt. York, edited by Tom Skeyhill. Cast: Joan Leslie, Walter Brennan, Margaret Wycherly, George Tobias, Ward Bond, June Lockhart, Howard da Silva, Noah Beery, Jr., Dickie Moore. Cooper received awards as best actor of 1941 from the New York Film Critics and the Motion Picture Academy.

54. BALL OF FIRE, A Goldwyn Production, released by RKO-Radio, 1941, *Howard Hawks*. Sp: Charles Brackett, Billy Wilder, b/o original story by Billy Wilder and Thomas Monroe. Cast: Barbara Stanwyck, Dana Andrews, Oscar Homolka, Richard Haydn, S.Z. Sakall, Henry Travers, Dan Duryea. Remade by Hawks as *A Song is Born* (1948), a musical version with Danny Kaye.

55. PRIDE OF THE YANKEES, A Goldwyn Production, released by RKO-Radio, 1942, *Sam Wood*. Sp: Jo Swerling, Herman J. Mankiewicz, b/o original story by Paul Gallico. Cast: Teresa Wright, Walter Brennan, Dan Duryea, Elsa Janssen, Ludwig Stossel, Babe Ruth.

56. FOR WHOM THE BELL TOLLS, Paramount, 1943, (c), *Sam Wood*. Sp: Dudley Nichols, b/o novel by Ernest Hemingway. Cast: Ingrid Bergman, Katina Paxinou, Akim Tamiroff, Arturo de Cordova, Vladimir Sokoloff, George Coulouris, Mikhail Rasumny, Lilo Yarson.

57. THE STORY OF DR. WASSELL, Paramount, 1944, (c), *Cecil B. DeMille*. Sp: Charles Bennett, Alan Le May, b/o story by James Hilton. Cast: Signe Hasso, Laraine Day, Dennis O'Keefe, Paul Kelly, Carl Esmond.

58. CASANOVA BROWN, An International Picture, released by RKO-Radio, 1944, *Sam Wood*. Sp: Nunnally Johnson, b/o play *Little Accident* by Floyd Dell and Thomas Mitchell. Cast: Teresa Wright, Frank Morgan, Patricia Collinge, Anita Louise, Mary Treen. Remake of *Little Accident* (1930) with Douglas Fairbanks, Jr. and ZaSu Pitts.

59. ALONG CAME JONES, An International Picture, released by RKO-Radio, 1945, *Stuart Heisler*. Sp: Nunnally Johnson, b/o story by Alan Le May. Cast: Loretta Young, Dan Duryea, William Demarest, Frank Sully, Russell Simpson.

60. SARATOGA TRUNK, Warners, 1945, *Sam Wood*. Sp: Casey Robinson, b/o novel by Edna Ferber. Cast: Ingrid Bergman, Flora Robson, Florence Bates, Jerry Austin, John Warburton.

61. CLOAK AND DAGGER, Warners, 1946, *Fritz Lang*. Sp: Albert Maltz, Ring Lardner, Jr., b/o story by Boris Ingster and John Larkin, suggested by a book by Corey Ford and Alastair MacBain. Cast: Lilli Palmer, Robert Alda, Vladimir Sokoloff, Helene Thimig, J. Edward Bromberg, Marjorie Hoshelle, Ludwig Stossel.

62. UNCONQUERED, Paramount, 1947, (c), *Cecil B. DeMille*. Sp: Jesse Lasky, Jr., Fredric M. Frank, Charles Bennett, b/o novel by Neil H. Swanson. Cast: Paulette Goddard, Boris Karloff, Howard da Silva, Ward Bond, C. Aubrey Smith, Henry Wilcoxon, Cecil Kellaway, Katherine DeMille.

63. GOOD SAM, RKO-Radio, 1948, *Leo McCarey*. Sp: Ken Englund, b/o story by Leo McCarey and John Klorer. Cast: Ann Sheridan, Ray Collins, Joan Lorring, Edmund Lowe, Louise Beavers, Dick Ross, Ruth Roman.

64. THE FOUNTAINHEAD, Warners, 1948, *King Vidor*. Sp: Ayn Rand, b/o her novel. Cast: Patricia Neal, Raymond Massey, Kent Smith, Henry Hull, Ray Collins, Moroni Olsen.

65. TASK FORCE, Warners, 1949, (c), *Delmer Daves*. Sp: Delmer Daves. Cast: Jane Wyatt, Walter Brennan, Wayne Morris, Julie London, Jack Holt, Bruce Bennett, Stanley Ridges.

66. BRIGHT LEAF, Warners, 1950, *Michael Curtiz*. Sp: Ranald MacDougall, b/o novel by Foster FitzSimons. Cast: Patricia Neal, Lauren Bacall, Jack Carson, Donald Crisp, Elizabeth Patterson.

67. DALLAS, Warners, 1950, (c), *Stuart Heisler*. Sp: John Twist. Cast: Ruth Roman, Steve Cochran, Raymond Massey, Barbara Payton, Antonio Moreno, Leif Erickson, Jerome Cowan.

68. YOU'RE IN THE NAVY NOW (U.S.S. TEAKETTLE), 20th Century-Fox, 1951, *Henry Hathaway*. Sp: Richard Murphy, from a *New Yorker* article by John W. Hazard. Cast: Jane Greer, Eddie Albert, Millard Mitchell, Jack Webb, Ray Collins, Charles Bronson, Richard Erdman, Jack Warden, Ed Begley, John McIntyre, Harvey Lembeck.

69. IT'S A BIG COUNTRY, MGM, 1951, *Clarence Brown* directed Cooper's sketch, with screenplay by Dorothy Kingsley. Also in the cast in other segments: Fredric March, Gene Kelly, Ethel Barrymore, William Powell, Janet Leigh, Marjorie Main, S.Z. Sakall, James Whitmore.

70. DISTANT DRUMS, Warners, 1951, (c), *Raoul Walsh*. Sp: Martin Rackin, Niven Busch, b/o story by Busch. Cast: Mari Aldon, Richard Webb, Arthur Hunnicutt, Robert Barrat.

71. HIGH NOON, United Artists, 1952, *Fred Zinnemann*. Sp: Carl Foreman, b/o story by John W. Cunningham. Cast: Grace Kelly, Katy Jurado, Lloyd Bridges, Thomas Mitchell, Otto Kruger, Lon Chaney, Jr., Lee Van Cleef. Cooper received his second Academy Award for this film.

72. SPRINGFIELD RIFLE, Warners, 1952, (c), *Andre De Toth*. Sp: Charles Marquis Warren, Frank Davis, b/o story by Sloan Nibley. Cast: Phyllis Thaxter, David Brian, Paul Kelly, Lon Chaney.

73. RETURN TO PARADISE, An Aspen Production, released by United Artists, 1953, (c), *Mark Robson*. Sp: Charles Kaufman, b/o book by James Michener. Cast: Roberta Haynes, Barry Jones, Moira MacDonald.

74. BLOWING WILD, Warners, 1953, *Hugo Fregonese*. Sp: Philip Yordan. Cast: Barbara Stanwyck, Anthony Quinn, Ruth Roman, Ward Bond.

75. GARDEN OF EVIL, 20th Century-Fox, 1954, (c), *Henry Hathaway*. Sp: Frank Fenton, b/o story by Fred Freiberger and William Tunberg. Cast: Susan Hayward, Richard Widmark, Cameron Mitchell, Hugh Marlowe, Rita Moreno.

76. VERA CRUZ, A Hecht-Lancaster Production, released by United Artists, 1954, (c), *Robert Aldrich*. Sp: James R. Webb, Ronald Kibbee, b/o story by Borden Chase. Cast: Burt Lancaster, Sarita Montiel, Denise Darcel, Cesar Romero, Ernest Borgnine, George Macready, Jack Elam.

77. THE COURT-MARTIAL OF BILLY MITCHELL, Warners, 1955, (c), *Otto Preminger*. Sp: Emmet Lavery, Milton Sperling, b/o their original story. Cast: Ralph Bellamy, Rod Steiger, Elizabeth Montgomery, Fred Clark, Charles Bickford, James Daly, Peter Graves, Charles Dingle.

78. THE FRIENDLY PERSUASION, Allied Artists, 1956, (c), *William Wyler*. Sp: (uncredited) by Michael Wilson, b/o book by Jessamyn West. Cast: Dorothy McGuire, Anthony Perkins, Marjorie Main, Richard Eyer, Phyllis Love, Robert Middleton, Walter Catlett, Mark Richman.

79. LOVE IN THE AFTERNOON, Allied Artists, 1957, *Billy Wilder*. Sp: Billy Wilder, I.A.L. Diamond, b/o novel *Ariane* by Claude Anet. Cast: Audrey Hepburn, Maurice Chevalier, John McGiver, Lise Bourdin.

80. TEN NORTH FREDERICK, 20th Century-Fox, 1958, *Philip Dunne*. Sp: Philip Dunne, b/o novel by John O'Hara. Cast: Geraldine Fitzgerald, Diane Varsi, Suzy Parker, Ray Stricklyn, Stuart Whitman, Tom Tully, John Emery, Barbara Nichols.

81. MAN OF THE WEST, A Mirisch Production, released by United Artists, 1958, (c), *Anthony Mann*. Sp: Reginald Rose, b/o novel by Will C. Brown. Cast: Julie London, Lee J. Cobb, Arthur O'Connell, Jack Lord, Royal Dano.

82. THE HANGING TREE, Warners, 1959, (c), *Delmer Daves*. Sp: Wendell Mayes, Halsted Welles, b/o novel by Dorothy M. Johnson. Cast: Maria Schell, Karl Malden, Ben Piazza, George C. Scott.

83. THEY CAME TO CORDURA, Columbia, 1959, (c), *Robert Rossen*. Sp: Ivan Moffat, Robert Rossen, b/o novel by Glendon Swarthout. Cast: Van Heflin, Rita Hayworth, Richard Conte, Tab Hunter, Dick York, Michael Callan, Robert Keith.

84. THE WRECK OF THE MARY DEARE, MGM, 1959, (c), *Michael Anderson*. Sp: Eric Ambler, b/o novel by Hammond Innes. Cast: Charlton Heston, Michael Redgrave, Emlyn Williams, Cecil Parker, Richard Harris, Alexander Knox, Virginia McKenna.

85. THE NAKED EDGE, A Seltzer-Glass Production, released by United Artists, 1961, *Michael Anderson*. Sp: Joseph Stefano, b/o novel *First Train to Babylon* by Max Ehrlich. Cast: Deborah Kerr, Eric Portman, Diane Cilento, Hermione Gingold, Peter Cushing, Michael Wilding, Wilfrid Lawson, Ronald Howard.

GUEST APPEARANCES

PARAMOUNT ON PARADE, Paramount, 1930. All-star musical with sketches directed by Dorothy Arzner, Rowland V. Lee and Edmund Goulding, among others. Cooper appears in modern sequence with Jack Oakie and Mary Brian and then in a musical number in period costume, shot in two-tone Technicolor, with Fay Wray, Richard Arlen, Jean Arthur, Virginia Bruce, *et. al*.

THE SLIPPERY PEARLS, 1932, A two-reeler sponsored by the Masquers Club for charity purposes. The all-star cast includes Norma Shearer, Irene Dunne, Laurel and Hardy, Loretta Young, Edward G. Robinson, Wallace Beery, Fay Wray, Barbara Stanwyck, Joan Crawford, Buster Keaton, *et. al*. Cooper plays a reporter in scene with Charles "Buddy" Rogers, William Haines and Eugene Pallette.

MAKE ME A STAR, Paramount, 1932, *William Beaudine*. Sp: Walter DeLeon, Arthur Kober and Sam Mintz. A version of *Merton of the Movies*, the book by Harry Leon Wilson, adapted for the stage by George S. Kaufman and Moss Hart. Cast: Stuart Erwin, Jóan Blondell, Zasu Pitts. Guest stars include Cooper, Tallulah Bankhead, Maurice Chevalier, Claudette Colbert, Fredric March, Sylvia Sidney, *et. al*.

HOLLYWOOD BOULEVARD, Paramount, 1936, *Robert Florey*. Sp: Marguerite Roberts, b/o story by Faith Thomas. Unbilled bit by Cooper in a cast headed by John Halliday, Marsha Hunt and Robert Cummings.

VARIETY GIRL, Paramount, 1947, *George Marshall*, Sp: Frank Tashlin, Robert Welch, Edmund Hartmann, Monte Brice. Cast: Mary Hatcher and Olga San Juan, with guest appearances by practically all the Paramount star roster, including Cooper, Stanwyck, Hope, Lamour, Crosby, Ladd, Goddard, *et. al*.

IT'S A GREAT FEELING, Warners, 1949, (c), *David Butler*. Sp: Jack Rose, Melville Shavelson. Cast: Doris Day, Dennis Morgan and Jack Carson with Warners contract players as themselves, including Cooper, Joan Crawford, Danny Kaye, Eleanor Parker, Patricia Neal, Edward G. Robinson, Jane Wyman, Ronald Reagan.

STARLIFT, Warners, 1951, *Roy Del Ruth*. Sp: John Klorer, Karl Kamb. Musical comedy about USO entertaining troops during the Korean War, with all-star cast including Cooper, James Cagney, Doris Day, Virginia Mayo, Ruth Roman, *et. al*.

ALIAS JESSE JAMES, A Hope Enterprises Production, released by United Artists, 1959, (c), *Norman McLeod*. Sp: William Bowers, D.D. Beauchamp. Cast: Bob Hope in a Western spoof with unbilled guest stars that include Cooper, Bing Crosby, Hugh O'Brian, James Arness, James Garner, *et. al*.

BIBLIOGRAPHY

Agee, James, *Agee on Film*. Beacon Press, Boston, 1958.

Baxter, John, *Hollywood in the Thirties*. A.S. Barnes & Co., New York, 1970.

Behlmer, Rudy (Ed.), *Memo from David O. Selznick*. The Viking Press, New York, 1972.

Bergman, Andrew, *We're in the Money*. New York University Press, New York, 1971.

Bogdanovich, Peter, *Fritz Lang in America*. Praeger, New York, 1967.

Bogdanovich, Peter, "Interview with Howard Hawks," *Cahiers du Cinema*, January, 1963.

Brown, Curtis F., *Ingrid Bergman*. Pyramid Publications, New York, 1973.

Canham, Kingsley, *The Hollywood Professionals*. A.S. Barnes & Co., New York, 1973.

Capra, Frank, *The Name Above the Title*. The Macmillan Company, New York, 1971.

Carpozi, Jr., George, *The Gary Cooper Story*. Arlington House, New Rochelle, 1970.

Casty, Alan, *The Films of Robert Rossen*. The Museum of Modern Art, New York, 1969.

Cobos, Juan and José Luis Pruneda, "Interview with Henry Hathaway," *Film Ideal*, March 15, 1964.

Corliss, Richard (Ed.), *The Hollywood Screenwriters*. Avon, New York, 1972.

Dickens, Homer, *The Films of Gary Cooper*. The Citadel Press, Secaucus, 1970.

Ferguson, Otis, *The Film Criticism of Otis Ferguson*. Temple University Press, Philadelphia, 1971.

"Gary Cooper": *Screen Greats Series No. 6*. Barven Publications, New York, 1972.

Goodman, Ezra, *The Fifty-Year Decline and Fall of Hollywood*. Simon and Schuster, New York, 1961.

Gow, Gordon, *Hollywood in the Fifties*. A.S. Barnes & Co., New York, 1971.

Greene, Graham, *Graham Greene on Film*. Simon and Schuster, New York, 1972.

Guiles, Fred Lawrence, *Marion Davies*. McGraw Hill, New York, 1972.

Higham, Charles and Joel Greenberg, *Hollywood in the Forties*. A.S. Barnes & Co., New York, 1968.

Kanin, Garson, *Remembering Mr. Maugham*. Atheneum, New York, 1966.

Lambert, Gavin, *On Cukor*. G.P. Putnam's Sons, New York, 1972.

Marion, Frances, *Off With Their Heads!* The Macmillan Company, New York, 1972.

Missiaen, J.C., *Anthony Mann*. Editions Universitaires, Paris, 1964.

Moullet, Luc and Michal Delahaye, "Interview with King Vidor." *Cahiers du Cinema*, October, 1962.

Munden, Kenneth W. (Ed.), *The American Film Institute Catalogue*. R.R. Bowker Company, New York & London, 1971.

Noames and Daney, "Interview with Leo McCarey." *Cahiers du Cinema*, February, 1965.

Nogueira, Rui, "Interview with Henry Hathaway." *Film in Focus* No. 7.

Osborne, Robert, *Academy Awards Illustrated*. Marvin Miller Enterprises, Hollywood, 1965.

Reid, John Howard, "The Next Best Second Fiddle: Henry Hathaway." *Films and Filming*, November, 1962.

Sarris, Andrew, *The American Cinema*. E.P. Dutton & Co., New York, 1968.

Sennett, Ted, *Warner Brothers Presents*. Arlington House, New Rochelle, 1971.

Shipman, David, *The Great Movie Stars: The Golden Years*. Crown Publishers, New York, 1970.

Silke, James R. and Michael Shamamian, *Rouben Mamoulian*. The American Film Institute, Washington, 1971.

Sternberg, Josef von, *Fun in a Chinese Laundry*. The Macmillan Company, New York, 1965.

Walker, Alexander, *Stardom*. Stein & Day, New York, 1970.

Wilk, Max, *The Wit and Wisdom of Hollywood*. Atheneum, New York, 1971.

Wood, Robin, *Howard Hawks*. Secker and Warburg Ltd., London, 1968.

INDEX

(Page numbers italicized indicate photographs)

157

ABOUT THE AUTHOR

René Jordan has written extensively on films for many publications, including *Film Quarterly*, *The Village Voice*, *Films in Review*, *Cinema*, and *Film Ideal*. He is the author of *Clark Gable* and *Marlon Brando*, two volumes in the Pyramid Illustrated History of the Movies. He lives in New York City.

ABOUT THE EDITOR

Ted Sennett is the author of *Warner Brothers Presents*, a survey of the great Warners films of the thirties and forties, and of *Lunatics and Lovers*, on the years of the "screwball" movie comedy. He has also written about films for magazines and newspapers. He lives in New Jersey with his wife and three children.